MY
CITY
HIGH
RISE
GAR
DEN

MY
CITY
HIGH
RISE
GAR
DEN

SUSAN
BROWNMILLER

New Brunswick, Camden, and
Newark, New Jersey, and London

Library of Congress Cataloging-in-Publication Data

Names: Brownmiller, Susan, author.
Title: My city highrise garden / Susan Brownmiller.
Description: New Brunswick, New Jersey : Rutgers University Press, [2017]
Identifiers: LCCN 2016046281| ISBN 9780813588896 (hardcover : alk.
paper) | ISBN 9780813588902 (e-book (epub)) | ISBN 9780813588919
(e-book (web pdf)) | ISBN 9780813591179 (e-book (mobi))
Subjects: LCSH: Urban gardening--New York (State)--New York--Anec-
dotes. | Roof gardening--New York (State)--New York--Anecdotes.
Classification: LCC SB453.2.N7 B76 2017 | DDC
635.09173/2097471--dc23
LC record available at https://lccn.loc.gov/2016046281

A British Cataloging-in-Publication record for this book is available
from the British Library.

∞The paper used in this publication meets the requirements of the
American National Standard for Information Sciences—Permanence of
Paper for Printed Library Materials, ANSI Z39.48–1992.

www.rutgersuniversitypress.org

Manufactured in the United States of America

CONTENTS

**MY
CITY
HIGH
RISE
GAR
DEN**

HELLO, TERRACE

I have been gardening in tubs and pots on a high terrace in a New York City apartment building for thirty-five years, unloading huge bags of soil every spring, battling the wind, fighting tiny life-sucking creatures, and crossing swords on occasion with an envious neighbor. I would have enjoyed gardening on a country estate, or at least on a lower floor, but I'm not complaining. I am lucky to have an outdoor space to pursue my passion, even if the harsh conditions twenty flights above street level are difficult for my plants.

Writers who garden like to tell how they acquired their patch—an inheritance of overgrown farmland and scrubby woods, that sort of thing. This is a New York story. It began in the 1960s when developers knocked down a block of tenements on the northwest edge of charming, historic Greenwich Village where it met a light-industry zone of meatpackers and factory lofts. The clunky redbrick ziggurat that rose on the site was so out of scale and character with the early Federal and Victorian row houses on the refined side of the border that horrified local preservationists went into action. They got the city to declare Greenwich Village a protected landmark with restrictions on the height on new construction.

The rogue behemoth, a fait accompli, had five terrace apartments on a penthouse floor. I can tell you that a penthouse used to be a single structure, but I can't fight real estate nomenclature or people's desires. New York is now home to residential towers with four—count 'em, four—designated penthouse floors. A private space with vines and flowers and a fabulous view is a big city dream, an enduring romantic fantasy of success at the top that owes a lot to old black-and-white Hollywood movies that were shot on fake sets.

Okay, I was renting a perfectly fine one-bedroom on the fifth floor of the behemoth that roused the preservationists when a book that I wrote made a lot of money. Understandably, my gaze turned upward. I asked Nestor, our hardworking superintendent, to let me know if a penthouse became available. My relationship with Nestor was very good. He admired my knack with houseplants. I never yelled when he forgot my request to fix something, unlike a famous actor in the building, known for his temper, who also wanted a penthouse. Nestor had a bad hip and his English was poor. This is relevant to my story. One day during a building workers' strike, he left the picket line and hobbled toward me in the lobby, shouting, "He died, he died!" It took me a while to figure out that Nestor was giving me a valuable tip and some crucial lead time to secure a suddenly available top-floor apartment. I gulped and grabbed at the chance, signed a lease that tripled my rent, and learned how to be a terrace gardener.

When I moved to my aerie in 1978, people weren't clamoring to live near a noisy meatpacking district that reeked of fat and blood and swarmed with flies. A wholesale bakery, an ice cream distributor, and a smelly frankfurter factory lay further west on my street. I remember the distinctive odor of an ink factory. Clanging boxcars that serviced the meatpackers shuttled back and forth on elevated tracks. At night, empty trucks parked near the closed West Side Highway—a portion had caved in—were a haven for anonymous sex. I never walked my dog in that direction in the evening.

Neighborhoods change. Mine went from a Wild West borderland to "hot." The highway reopened with a riverside park running alongside it, and the meatpackers gave way to trendy nightclubs, designer boutiques, condominium towers of glass, and destination dining. The shuttling

Bucolic!

boxcars are gone; a large section of the elevated tracks was torn down, and the rest was transformed into the artfully landscaped High Line, a destination for tourists from around the world. Most recently, one of the city's museums built its new site near the waterfront. My building went co-op in the mid-1980s, but 30 percent of us remained as rent-stabilized tenants under state law. I couldn't afford to buy at the offering price, or at any subsequent price in the crazily spiraling real estate market.

Now I'll say it: My penthouse has sweeping views of the Hudson River, the ever-changing configurations of lower Manhattan and the Jersey shoreline, and picture-postcard sunsets. I follow the phases of the moon and can spot the Big Dipper even though bright city lights obscure the night sky. Most visitors don't notice my garden when they step out on the terrace. "Wow, what a view!" they exclaim when I want to show them a daylily.

Such is the ego of a high-terrace gardener: enormous. It has to be enormous to overcome a hostile, unnatural environment. My terrace is exposed to the elements on three sides. Instead of earth under my feet, I have dun-colored pavers and metal drains. The wind is my unwanted companion. I have a super-abundance of sun and little shade. Like gardeners everywhere, I am grateful for rain, until a freak spring or summer comes along that is nothing but rain. All my hopes and dreams for luxuriant growth are rooted in tubs and pots that can dry out fearfully in one hot summer day. I drag around a hose, unkinking the kinks, because an automatic watering system (trust me, I had one) does not substitute for a vigilant human being.

Being at one with nature in the sense of Emerson and Thoreau doesn't apply to a zigzag three-sided terrace that I can stroll from end to end and back again in seventy-five seconds. Not hurrying, and not looking at anything but my stopwatch. (I did this once for research.) Here are the dimensions of my outdoor space as measured by me with my yardstick: seven and a half feet wide on the short north side, where I grow hydrangea and honeysuckle and where I keep my garden tools in a shed beneath an overhang; nine feet wide on the long west side, where I have roses, coreopsis, a bench, and a large table and chairs; a mere four and a quarter feet wide on the most favorable south side—more roses, daylilies, and a butterfly bush—that ends at the railing of a neighbor's terrace. At the height of my giddiest ambitions, the zigzag corners were home to three birch trees, a dwarf peach, and a flowering crabapple, while Boston ivy and a climbing rose covered a fair portion of the brick walls.

Structural renovations of the building's façade, which take place periodically around here, have caused horrible setbacks to my garden. For three summers I lost all daytime access when the terrace was commandeered as the staging area for various work crews and their guy wires and pulleys and vats of tar. The ivy was torn from the brick walls; my climbing rose was cut down. The huge wood tubs that held my trees were moved hither and yon until the tubs and trees were unceremoniously hacked apart and trashed. I would sneak out at sundown when the work crews were gone, slip under the guy wires to avoid being garroted, and water what remained of my treasures. My agony and frustrations during the bad times were always countered by my determined resolve to make my garden beautiful again.

The worst of my challenges was the winter of 2014–2015, the Northeast's coldest in sixty-five years, a relentless assault of snowstorms, rainstorms, and ice storms that was followed by a depressing non-spring of thaws and freezes. Weather was a major news story up and down the East Coast. I was proud that I managed to survive without sliding into a snowbank and breaking a wrist, but when I finally ventured onto the terrace, which I hadn't given any thought to for months, it was clear that many of my favorite plants had succumbed. I had just turned eighty, and the prospect of starting over in the garden was particularly daunting.

I had no choice. I started over. I wasn't ready to go down in humiliation and defeat.

Yes, I have a private oasis in a competitive city, a place to dig and plant, to putter, to water, feed and prune, to step back (carefully) and admire my efforts from limited angles, but I wouldn't call it an oasis of peace. It is an ongoing challenge in an unnatural environment. I still find it astonishing that my green space lures so many creatures of nature: migratory butterflies and birds are at the top of the list; aphids and ants and bees are at the bottom. I notice that I'm always smiling when I do my toughest chores. In truth, I smile all the time on my terrace, and I'm generally doing a chore. Although I am not a spiritual person, my garden has given me many moments of pure exaltation: pulling a carrot out of the soil; drawing down a ripe peach; listening to the nightly clack and hum of crickets during their fall mating season; a morning greeting from a newly unfurled rose.

New technology has transformed my gardening habits. Polyurethane containers gradually replaced my made-to-order redwood boxes that did not last for a lifetime as promised. A lightweight, sterile potting mix shot through with perlite is now my all-purpose planting medium, ending a long association with wriggling earthworms. I surf the proliferating websites devoted to gardening and note that they are often more useful than my library of weighty reference books. Nowadays I generally locate, order, and pay for a new plant with a couple of clicks, though nothing beats browsing through the printed catalogs that come by mail. I crease the page corners, stick in Post-its, circle what I want with a highlight marker, and seal the deal in a friendly chat by phone with a live person. May there always be live persons! And I never tire of reading books about other people's gardens.

My garden engages me intellectually and emotionally. It is a never-ending challenge because something is always bound to go wrong. Ah, but when things go right. . . .

WIND

Abreezy hilltop or a windswept seacoast lulled by deceptive interludes of peace and calm: these difficult habitats are the best comparisons I can make to a high city terrace. On blustery days when I'd rather be indoors, I can see that my plants aren't having a good time either. Wind is my garden's main enemy, a force of nature highrise gardeners must develop strategies against if one is to have a garden at all.

A strong wind dries out the moisture in a plant's leaves and overburdens the normal transpiration process—the hydraulic uplift that draws water and nutrients from the roots to the stems and ultimately to the leaves that depend on the process. If moisture evaporates from the leaves faster than it can be replenished, the result will be parched, torn, brown, shriveled leaves that are dead by any description. Swirling wind currents cause additional mayhem. A powerful gust can snap the rigid stem of a tall flowering plant, break the hold of a vine, lop off the lower branch of a woody shrub, and twist an upright evergreen conifer over the years into a misshapen form that is really ugly. I've seen this happen.

Wind can desiccate buds, shred flowers, and topple a tree. Wind plays havoc with a normally tenacious vine like Boston ivy whose tendrils are supposed to cling to a brick wall. Wind has the mischievous power to unhook the carefully twisted ties that support the lax canes of a climbing rose. Wind can slam my terrace doors shut with a loud bang that loosens the hinges. Wind can stop me from stepping out on the terrace because the force is so strong that I can't push the door open. One afternoon I saw my neighbor across the way cowering on her knees in a corner of her terrace—she had been felled by a sudden gust.

This is nothing to boast about, but New York is windier than Chicago, the so-called Windy City. New York's prevailing winds usually come from the west—northwest in winter changing to southwest during the gardening months. Calm weather at street level is no indicator of conditions higher up. Even a lightly blowing wind will scurry up the sides of tall buildings and gain velocity across rooftops and exposed terraces.

During my novice gardening years when I planted spring bulbs, I observed to my annoyance that the tulips in public parks and in the little fenced areas under the street trees flowered two weeks earlier than mine. When my laggards colored up, their wind-tossed stems flopped over in a heap. I stopped growing tulips. My crabapple blossomed later than the crabapples at street level; my birch trees gave me terrifying moments when their chained tubs rocked and rolled. According to the maps that are issued by the U.S. Department of Agriculture, New York City is in hardiness zone 7b, a most pleasant climate for an extensive range of trees, shrubs, flowering plants, fruits, and vegetables, but the breezy altitude up here puts my garden in a turbulent and chillier microclimate that is not marked on the map. Everything I plant is cleared for the colder zone 6, to be on the safe side.

I used to yearn for a walled garden because I've seen them on majestic estates in England and France—usually they wall in fruit and vegetable plots—but that idea wouldn't work. First, it wouldn't be permitted, and second, I'd lose my precious view. Third, a walled garden is not a wind deterrent. My terrace perimeter has a low brick wall topped by a wrought-iron railing for a total height of four feet that satisfies the city's building safety codes. This is high enough to keep a person from

Quercifolia hydrangea

accidentally falling off, but it cannot prevent a strong wind from doing its damage.

Britain's Royal Horticultural Society reports that wind deflected by a solid brick wall will rise and spill over the wall in a snarl of eddies; I can attest to those downdrafts. And it turns out that the true purpose of walled gardens in the Victorian age was to keep out animals and poachers. It is true that a permeable barrier composed of an evergreen needle-leafed hedge, such as the yew, will slow the wind down. The Royal Horticultural Society proposes three staggered rows of yews for a really effective barrier. What city terrace has space for that? The single bank of yews I once kept on the north side of my terrace obscured my view and didn't leave much room for things I really want to grow.

One obvious strategy is to search for plants that are known for their wind resistance, or more accurately, for their tolerance of windy conditions. Thin needle evergreens like the yew can tolerate wind; however, broadleaf evergreens, like rhododendron and azaleas, will succumb to wind damage. Hydrangeas and shrub roses that do well near the seaside fit the bill. Another approach is to scour the catalogs for shorter hybrids of old-timey favorites. Hybridizers are working diligently to produce smaller varieties of popular plants to accommodate today's smaller gardens. Plenty of moderate-size daylilies are available for a high terrace, and some moderate-size irises as well, although the iris season is very brief and then you've got a pot with iris blades and no flowers for the rest of the spring and summer.

Just seeing the word "dwarf" in a catalog makes my heart flutter. Happy was the day when I found a ten-inch goldenrod. I almost gave up waiting for a dwarf hollyhock, and guess what? Dwarf hollyhocks—well, hollyhocks that are three feet high not counting their pot—have been introduced, but not yet in all the myriad hollyhock colors. Hollyhocks are supposed to be tall and blowsy leaning against a high fence in a yard; I haven't got a high fence or a yard, but I do buy and enjoy tending one new short hollyhock in a pot every year.

It's crucial that I put a limit on stem height for my flowering perennials and annuals, and choose the shorter varieties of drought-resistant plants for my garden, if there are shorter varieties. Campanula and penstemon have short varieties but there's no point in considering delphiniums—nobody's bred a short one yet. Two feet is my preferred maximum height in a flower stem; taller stems are liable to snap in the wind. "Wiry" is another descriptive word that draws my attention when I look through a catalog. A short wiry stem, characteristic of thread-leaf coreopsis and some anemones, will simply dance in the wind.

My major strategy is liberal watering. Windblown plants that lose moisture through surface evaporation, making their systems work double-time to keep up with the pace, will dry out the soil in their tubs in no time flat. One generous rainfall is not sufficient to saturate the parched soil. New York City is blessed with plenty of rain—forty-four inches in an average year—but a terrace garden of tubs and pots on an artificial surface cannot take full advantage of every welcome burst from the sky, as a yard garden does. Rain that drums on my textured pavers simply flows toward my terrace drains. (Beware of clogged drains.) I water my prize possession, the 'Nikko Blue' hydrangea, daily in the heat of summer. There is no mystery to this hydrangea's needs— it collapses like a corseted fainting lady in a *fin de siècle* ballroom if I'm not quick with the hose.

Karel Čapek, the Czech playwright, treated readers to a comic diatribe about his tribulations with his hose in *The Gardener's Year*, a compilation of newspaper essays he wrote from the vantage point of his spacious yard in Prague: "It refreshes you enormously if you squirt with the nozzle against the wind; it is almost a water cure when it drenches you quite through. A hose has also a special predilection for developing a hole somewhere in the middle, where you expect it least; and there you are standing like a god of water in the midst of sparkling jets with a long snake coiled at your feet; it is an overwhelming sight. When you are wet to the skin you contentedly declare that the garden has had enough, and you go get dry. In the meantime the garden said 'Ouf,' lapped up your water without a wink, and is as dry and thirsty as it was before." I can relate to that.

When I started my garden, I installed an automatic watering system of PVC pipes and thin rubber feeders for the main containers on the terrace, but I always supplemented the Rube Goldberg contraption (they're less intrusive today) with a watering can and a hose. The pipes for my automatic watering system were dismantled during one of the building's pointing and bricking operations and I never had them replaced, but I've sure had my share of kinks and tangles and leaks with my hundred-foot hose, not to mention tripping on it when I've been too lazy to spool it back on the reel. Listen, I am grateful to have an outdoor spigot that connects to the inside bathroom plumbing; most terrace gardeners are not so privileged. I am also privileged to live in a city that has never had a serious water crisis, thanks to our plentiful upstate reservoirs.

On a social note, a light wind can wreck my plans for a dinner party al fresco that was supposed to be a delightful evening of urbane sophistication. The meal is ready, the guests are seated, but they look uneasy. A sudden breeze has come up! I can't blame my guests for not wanting to eat and drink in a wind tunnel with the tablecloth flapping. Twice I've been stopped in my tracks before I'd even set the table; this happened when friends confessed to a fear of heights and refused point blank to step onto the terrace. It's amazing how many high-functioning achievers suffer from vertigo and a palpable terror of hurtling into the abyss. If I pull off two or three evenings of outdoor dining during a summer, I consider that to be an excellent record. Needless to say, there are plenty of evenings when conditions are perfect for dining outdoors; however, those marvelous nights when the air is still and the visibility is crystal clear and the city and the river are looking magnificent and it's thrilling to see the moon over Manhattan generally aren't the evenings when I've planned in advance to throw a dinner party.

THE BIRCHES

One month after moving into my penthouse, it dawned on me that adept as I was with indoor plants, I was clueless about how to organize the empty stretch of concrete my dreams had focused on. The terrace needed professional help.

I made a panicky call to D., a highly regarded landscape architect who lived in a townhouse down the street with a precisely designed shade garden. D. came over to survey the site and lost no time in laying out the big picture. The dining area could go *here*, a sunning area with recliners could go *there*. Roses might work on the south side. Boston ivy, trained correctly, could cover the brick walls, and a colorful row of short mixed annuals was an obvious choice for the western flank that faced the river. Trees were a possibility if I cared to go in that direction, and I might want a privacy hedge at the two ends of the terrace to mark off my space.

My head was spinning. D. had said trees. My father had inherited an etching of birch trees—if there was one tree I could recognize, at least on paper, it was the birch (genus *Betula*) with its slender trunk, white bark, slightly drooping branches, and small, pointed leaves. Birches are celebrated in poems and folksongs. Birches are pioneer trees in northern forests. Birches flourish in Siberia. I wondered if they would survive on a Manhattan terrace.

"Excuse me, you said trees. Could I have birches?"

D. narrowed his eyes at the zigzag corners that faced the river. "Yes, you could have three, almost a grove. You might even get some shade.

Betula

I don't recommend an awning, but you should consider an automatic watering system or you'll be married to your terrace."

"You're saying I can have birches?"

D. was crisply efficient in those days, a romantic perfectionist. I could not have started my garden without him. On this beautiful sunlit day he mentioned a nursery on Canal Street that could send over young birch clumps, and he recommended a water tank company that made junior-size tubs to hold trees.

"Hold on, I have a distant relative in the water tank business!" In the 1890s, my grandfather Abraham on my mother's side, a barrel maker from Minsk, had done well for himself in New York with a new way to install water pumps and wood storage tanks on the roofs of buildings. He was thirty-two when he died in a shop accident the family never talked about. From a wedding photograph, I know he was very handsome. My grandmother Dora, suddenly a widow with two

14

sons and three daughters, waved off competitors who urged her to sell; she put her mother, Sarah, in charge of the children and went to work managing the office side of the business. When her sons Murray and Joe were old enough to replace her, the company became theirs. A slim connection to water tanks in my family history was worth a phone call.

The distant relative I'd never met responded with a grand gesture; he must have known the long-ago family stories. His team arrived with three steel-ringed oak tubs, thick and sturdy, three feet high and wide, and hoisted them over the rooftop. He waved off any payment. Guys from the Canal Street nursery came by with soil and young birch clumps, their root balls wrapped in burlap. They plunked the trees into the tubs, tethered the trunks to the parapet corners and anchored the tubs themselves to the corners with chains. After the guys finished the tethering and anchoring, the trees and I were on our own.

The birches grew taller and fuller, their slender branches and pointy green leaves fluttered against the sky. I fed them with Miracle-Gro and watered them daily, tapering off in the fall when the leaves turned yellow and dropped. Pale green catkins dangled on the branches every spring, attempting to pollinate and colonize in the natural order of things, as if that reproductive feat, so easy for a birch in a normal environment, could be accomplished in a paved concrete city. When I strolled around the neighborhood and looked up at my trees, I felt the pride of possession. My flags, so to speak, were waving. I had defined my space, marked my territory, nurtured arboreal life where it never had been before.

Nature's creatures from the wider world took notice. Baltimore orioles and red cardinals stopped by. Blue jays alighted in the branches, cawing loudly. Migrating sapsuckers—*rat-tat-tat*—drilled neat rows of holes in the white bark. (After they returned for several years, I began to wish they wouldn't.) Some type of insect I instinctively feared gained a hold in one of the trees, spinning three lumpy grey cocoons that looked like the work of demented witches. What desperate species would make its home in such a precarious spot? Not caring to find out, I dislodged the cocoons with a broom, wrapped the webby mess in newspapers and sent the bundle down the compactor chute. (Years later, I determined that the cocoons had been the work of the Baldfaced hornet, known for its poor choices.)

As the birches soared and extended their branches I never did get any shade, but I noticed the chained tubs had begun to rock in a gusty wind. In a howler the tubs strained and shimmied, making me nervous. Obviously the birches had become too dense for the wind to flow through, and the only solution was to top off the trees and thin the branches. I bought a ladder and a long-pole pruner. More often than I care to remember I'd climb into a tub, brace my body against a trunk, and grab a branch to make a cut. The trick was never to look down.

Hurricane Gloria nicked Manhattan in September 1985. I taped the windows, closed the blinds, got under the covers and covered my ears against the whining and thudding. The damage was one tree down, prostrate across the length of the terrace. Evidently the weight of the tub and the height of the parapet had kept the birch from going airborne and sailing over the edge. I examined my fallen giant and took the opportunity to remove some broken branches. Then I alerted the building staff whose impressive teamwork heaved the tree upright again.

Should one fallen tree have served as sufficient warning? It didn't. Years later a freak wind toppled another birch that had to be righted. I happily resumed my chores of watering, feeding, topping off, and thinning to keep my arbor green and healthy, though I discontinued one crucial job that had become too hard to handle. I'd been warned that if I didn't dig into the soil and prune their roots on an annual basis the birches would become root-bound in their homes. Now the water I lovingly gave them sat on the surface for an eternity (maybe one hour) before it was absorbed.

My trees were living on borrowed time; the surprise end came in the form of a delegation from the building's management. Very politely, afraid I'd create a terrible scene, I was informed of an upcoming renovation: my terrace had to be cleared so its poured concrete surface could be replaced with a new lining and textured pavers. Some of my small containers could be stored on a neighbor's terrace during the overhaul but there was no way to move the formidable birch tubs. They would have to be trashed.

I lit a cigarette like Marlene Dietrich facing the firing squad and said, "Okay."

My life with birches had lasted twenty-five years, a respectable span for a tree on a city terrace. During this quarter-century my dog had died, my cat had died, the man I'd been living with had gone elsewhere, and D., my brilliant landscape architect, had lost his life in a fire. I had grown used to departures.

The textured pavers were a great improvement over the poured concrete. After mourning for the trees and staring at their empty spaces, I made a sensible plan to bring in polyurethane tubs and fill them with low roses.

THE CHORES OF MARCH

My garden comes alive in March. The great awakening takes place despite a freak snowstorm, below-average temperatures, or rainy weeks on end when the sun does not shine. That's nature. The days are longer, and the plant world reacts accordingly. Taking my cue from this unstoppable spring miracle, I spring to life too. March signals "get going," and I answer the call.

Calendars are no help—there isn't a fixed day in the month when March puts forth its toots and flares. March is notoriously unpredictable, a truculent lover full of hints and promises. My plants are stirring. Ours is a cooperative venture, so I wait for a day of relative warmth and calm, when the wind isn't whipping my face, to throw off my winter jacket and get to work. I'm in this game of spring renewal for necessity as well as for pleasure. My plants need me.

Two penthouse gardens in my field of vision have crews of professional gardeners already on the job. One is a duplex condo that has changed ownership many times. I remember the friendly hippie who rented the small upper level before the two floors became a duplex; a flowerchild of the sixties, she tended chance seedlings that floated into her space. The big lower terrace is a wraparound. It now sports a solarium with a domed roof, and the small upper terrace is now an arbor covered in vines. When a celebrity buzz app reported that the movie star Jennifer Aniston had bought the double-decker *and was in the building*, fifty of her excited fans brandishing iPhones massed behind police barriers on the street. They hoped to catch the star as she left the front entrance to enter her limo. I know this because I happened to be walking to the subway and asked a cop what the ruckus was about. There goes the neighborhood, I thought. Aniston sold quickly to a mystery owner who does not attract amateur paparazzi.

It's a different world up here, one that not many people get to see because they'd need a high vantage point like mine. Approximately thirty patios, balconies, and rooftop gardens of various sizes lie between the river and me; the commitment to intensive gardening varies from rooftop to rooftop and from terrace to terrace. The roof gardens on the brownstones are elegantly designed. Some of the terrace occupants are content with a few higgledy-piggledy plants. One rooftop I'd grown rather familiar with over the years used to be covered in Astroturf with a raised wood deck and a barbecue grill at the far end; I see that the roof is being resurfaced, a common New York experience. I hope that when the waterproofing job is finished, the roof will be shared again by the folks who used to go up there.

My behemoth apartment building has lots of terraces on its setbacks, and the co-op board finally sprang for a professionally landscaped rooftop forty years after the original developer promised one in his prospectus. I have to say that the 360-degree view from the co-op's garden is superior to mine, and the co-op's budget for landscaping and maintenance is superior too. Insert a smiley emoticon here.

It's wonderful that these outdoor spaces are multiplying above the hurly-burly of the city. They are a testament to people's need for a private refuge outside the confines of their apartment walls and to the restorative powers of fresh air, a sunrise or sunset, and an unlikely oasis for living plants.

Purple shoots are peeping out of the soil in the *Dicentra* tub. Pulling out last year's dead stalks is an easy project. Bleeding Heart, aka *Dicentra spectabilis*, never fails me. Arching stems of pendulous heart-shaped pink flowers with white tassels will be the first blooms I'll have, and the show will happen fast. Robert Fortune, one of a rugged breed of

Parsley

eighteenth- and nineteenth-century European plant hunters to hit the jackpot in Asia, found this plant on the Chinese island of Chusan after the Opium Wars and shipped it to London; within a few years Bleeding Heart, initially dubbed Lady's Heart or Lady's Locket, became a beloved favorite in British cottage gardens and across this country. The graceful plant is really too sweet, pink, and puffy to be called "bleeding." My Bleeding Heart grows on the shadier north side of my terrace where I can see it from my kitchen and dining room windows. It suffers rough moments when it is whipped by the wind, usually when it's blooming, but it is a champion survivor. When it goes dormant after its breathtaking early spring display, I drag the tub to an even shadier spot to give the plant a well-deserved rest.

Taxonomists gave the Bleeding Heart a new Latinate family name a few years ago. Excited by new DNA sequencing, they reclassified the plant from *Dicentra spectabilis* to *Lamprocapnos spectabilis*, an unpronounceable clumsy mouthful for sure. Commercial growers and distributors have adopted a wait-and-see approach to the name change, and garden bloggers have expressed outright indignation. One blogger wrote, "It was called *Dicentra* for 150 years and it'll be called *Dicentra* for another 150 years." Take that, taxonomists, whoever you are.

The saw-toothed leaves of a dwarf salvia and the whorled, fleshy leaves of a dwarf sedum are emerging. These plants require my hand to clear away last fall's dead foliage—more easy tasks. Onward to my many pots of daylilies, where slender green leaves are poking through the tangled, limp, grey detritus of last year's leaves. I'll tease out the encircling mass of dead stuff in the daylily pots, their natural mulch, when the strands yield easily to a slight tug.

I must pluck and use the fresh clump of parsley before it dies. Parsley is a biennial that makes a strong appearance at the beginning of its second year before it gives up the ghost and must be chucked. A prayer in the Passover Haggadah blesses the parsley as a sign of spring's renewal, and the leader of the Seder picks up the greens and proclaims, "Behold the parsley!" I love the moment when the humble parsley is held aloft and blessed.

More in the herbs department. The chives have come back, and so has the sorrel. Chives are always useful, and once in a while I make sorrel soup. Both plants need clearing away of dead matter at the soil line. No problem.

A pansy overwintered. This is a news bulletin! I always thought pansies were short-season annuals. Last spring my neighbor Christine left three little pretties in starter pots at the door; the magenta pansy with dark blotches outperformed the others by blooming through the summer and fall. I pinched off the spent blooms and was surprised to see it flower sporadically through the winter. Now the pansy is sporting fresh blooms. Apparently some pansies can perform as biennials (who knew?). 'Magenta Xtreme', as I call it, is having a fine spring flush before it is doomed to expire. 'Xtreme' has company—a yellow pansy was left at the door a few days ago by my neighbor Dan. My penthouse floor neighbors are determined to keep me in pansies.

My roses. Pinkish-red nubbins, like pimples, are swelling on the canes, holding the certainty of leaves. The roses on the south side have actually leafed out. March is marching time for my roses. This is the time to grab my pruning shears and lop off the dried flowers and wrinkled hips that remained on the shrubs from last fall. Then I'll remove the shriveled, discolored wood that did not survive the winter, and after that I'll remove the inward-growing branches that are crossing and rubbing each other. When a rose bush breaks out of dormancy in spring, it should be pruned to have an open center. New crossovers and tangles will be dealt with during the summer as they appear. This year all my roses returned with vigor. Last spring I had several goners that required extracting their dead root masses from their tubs.

Whoa—the butterfly bush, my lavender buddleia with orange eyes. Every March the three-foot arching 'Nanho Purple' that delighted me and the butterflies the previous summer gets an early jump on my spring pruning intentions. Wasting its energy, I'd say, the buddleia unfurls grey-blue leaves along the length of its branches. This is so wrong! Nature's relaxed plan for the plant, which always catches me off guard, will produce a tall, rangy, unkempt shrub. My job is to whack the whole thing back to six inches, a severe procedure that will encourage new growth from the base. I'm on the case with my Felco pruners and a Japanese cross-tooth saw. After a minute of hesitation—can nature really be so wrong, or rather, so mindless of the human esthetic?—I confidently begin to slice and saw.

A quick check on the irises 'Batik' and 'Ruffled Velvet' and the one whose name I've forgotten. These are "specimen plants" for me, fated to be grown in solitary containers, because one iris per pot is all

I have room for. Who plants just one iris per pot? A terrace gardener, that's who. I rarely allocate space for popular beauties that bloom only in spring, and bloom briefly at that, but after a lifetime of buying cut stems at flower shops, I'd hankered for an iris experience of my own. The iris blades are looking strong. Wait a second—where's 'Ruffled Velvet'? Oh, over there.

Solidago 'Little Lemon', an eighteen-inch goldenrod bred in Israel that I planted on the north side five autumns ago, is coming up slowly. Based on last year's flower spikes—August is goldenrod's prime flowering month—I'll move the tub a few feet so the wee goldenrod can catch the lazy afternoon rays of the spring sun.

Okay, a difficult chore. I take a close look at my favorite hydrangea, 'Nikko Blue', that has been in recovery mode for two years because of the odd weather patterns that afflicted the city. I inspect it for winterkill; 'Nikko' shows me its viable buds and the ones that are hopelessly shriveled. Its giant urn is in a zigzag corner that I can't walk around, so I lean in gently to work on the outlying branches. Then I get out my eight-foot pruning pole with cords on a pulley to reach in further. The pulley's cords often tangle, making me worry that I'll lose control over the pole. Once 'Nikko''s buds begin to swell and unfurl they can be knocked off accidentally. And they often are.

New growth is so tender.

The field of coreopsis that borders my western flank is still dormant, but it's too soon to worry. *Coreopsis verticillata* is slow to send up its green starbursts from its spreading roots, but when it does I'll twist and yank out last year's dead stalks. This chore is not pleasant. So many dead stalks and so many emerging green starbursts that I can wrench out accidentally if I'm not careful.

On the south side, the wine-colored shoots of the peony 'Edulis Superba' are piercing the soil. I will tease out last year's dead stalks and work a layer of dehydrated cow manure into the peony's container as soon as the new shoots grow and green up. I'll fill up the rose tubs with a fresh layer of topsoil. I'll add some fresh soil to the daylily tubs too. Meanwhile I'll do some sweeping. It's amazing how many pockets of dead leaves, scraps of plastic, and torn paper accumulate behind my containers during the winter.

I pass the climbing rose again and notice a few perky green sprouts popping up where they don't belong. Out they go, these invaders, whatever they are or could become. Weeding is an automatic, almost unconscious process. See it, pull it. No groveling on the ground on all fours as yard gardeners must do; the height of my containers makes weeding a relatively easy chore. It's uncanny how some weeds resemble the emerging shoots of the perennials I lovingly tend. I need to check the daylilies, campanula, and the coreopsis most carefully for imposters. Imposter weeds, as I call them, are the most gratifying to pull, my best gotcha moments.

Oh, no! A high branch of the climber has come loose from the wall. The nail heads are in place but what happened to the plastic ties? A branch waving free of its moorings is a frequent catastrophe for a climbing rose that is buffeted by the wind. Retying it requires that I drag my rickety tall ladder from the shed below the overhang on the north side, situate it carefully against the wall on the south side in a way that does not crush the rose's emerging leaves, and climb as close as I can get to my target without losing my balance. I've never yet lost my balance on this old wood ladder but I don't care to perform the tricky feat today. Okay, I'll do it tomorrow. I really should do it today.

Ouch, I grabbed the wood ladder and now I've got deep splinters in my palm and fingers. I should have gotten rid of this ladder years ago. I'll call Barney's Hardware and have them deliver a fiberglass ladder this evening if they can. I hope some long soaks in Epsom salts will bring my splinters to the surface.

Damn it, this is no time to obsess about splinters. Another crisis demands my immediate attention. I've been toiling in the garden for hours and only now I see that several of the pots and tubs are perilously dry. The hose is lying curled in the shed, where I stored it for winter near the rickety ladder. Connecting the hose is definitely a task for tomorrow: it must be unreeled and attached to the outside spigot that connects through the brick wall to a riser pipe in the bathroom. Today I'll fill my watering can at the kitchen faucet and traipse through the apartment, many times, bearing the life-sustaining gift in my hand.

March makes me so happy. Here is a salute from Emily Dickinson, the great reclusive poet—and gardener—of Amherst, Massachusetts:

> Dear March—Come in—
> How glad I am—
> I hoped for you before—
> Put down your Hat—
> You must have walked—
> How out of Breath you are—
> Dear March, how are you, and the Rest—
> Did you leave Nature well—
> Oh March, Come right upstairs with me—
> I have so much to tell—

A joyous poem in Dickinson's unconventional punctuation that expresses my sentiments exactly. Except that sometimes March does not come until late April, and sometimes in late May.

A WATER FEATURE

At country estates, landscape designers often propose a "water feature" for visual interest, lively motion, and calming sounds. The options include dredging and filling a pond or a lake, or perhaps creating a stepped waterfall and a brook. A fountain that recycles its water is recommended for a small city garden. My garden's water feature is a great stretch of the Hudson River that I am privileged to see from my terrace.

As it flows past the island of Manhattan, the Hudson forms a geographical boundary between New York and New Jersey and gives me a nodding acquaintance with the mushrooming skylines of Hoboken and Jersey City. On their side of the river, Jersey folks see Manhattan's skyline from their perspective. If I look north, I can still catch a glimpse of the Palisades, the rocky cliffs formed in the Triassic era, though they are increasingly obscured by highrises on both sides of the Hudson.

Looking south, I follow the river as it widens and pours into the gleaming upper bay of New York Harbor, once the heart of the commercial Port of New York and New Jersey. A small island in the bay belongs to "The Lady," the name air traffic controllers and harbormasters bestowed on the Statue of Liberty. No other sight has inspired more hope, extended such grave assurance of protection, or is more unconventionally beautiful than her singular presence, her torch held high to welcome immigrants who made the long Atlantic passage to better their lives. My view of America's freedom icon is fairly distant. I can make out her uplifted arm and torch, her spiked helmet and the folds of her skirt, and supply the details of her vigilant gaze and worried brow from postcards and memory. Even on days of poor visibility, I feel reassured that The Lady is commanding the harbor. Beyond the curve of the shore, past my vista, the Hudson concludes the journey it began upstate in Adirondack mountain streams by joining the East River and other urban waterways to flow into the Atlantic Ocean.

Manhattan's waterfront does not bear much resemblance to the active port it used to be. Luxury ocean liners and their terminals started to dwindle in the latter half of the twentieth century when jets became the quick, affordable way to travel. In another blow, the automated docks of Newark Bay lured container shipping from Manhattan's labor-intensive cargo piers. During this same half-century, the Hudson acquired a deserved reputation for being polluted and stinky, a disaster area of industrial waste, PCBs, dead fish, lost spawning grounds, and raw sewage. The Left's folk-singing hero Pete Seeger found a new cause in cleaning up the river; his sloop the *Clearwater* was an inspiration for other environmental activists who created a tidal wave of lawsuits to enlighten government thinking about the stewardship of rivers and aquatic life.

Today the largest vessels that ply a much cleaner river are the brightly painted, multi-decked cruise ships of the Norwegian, Carnival, Holland America, and Princess lines that depart from midtown terminals to take passengers on short Caribbean holidays. The cruise ships alert smaller craft to their presence by a sonorous blast that makes me stop whatever I'm doing to watch them pass. For a while Disney had ships that tooted "When You Wish upon a Star" in the halting meter of a kid playing a church organ.

Smaller boats move up, down, and across the blue-grey water, leaving their own white wake. Circle Line and Spirit of New York tour boats glide past the many hulking skylines of Manhattan, squat commuter ferries chug to and from Staten Island, excursion boats take sightseers to Ellis and Liberty Islands. I see oil tankers and cement barges accompanied by tugs; private yachts and fishing boats; billowing white sailboats; yellow water taxis; outriggers, kayaks, and canoes; and preening fireboats that are testing their sprays. Sleek, fiberglass "cigarette boats" race by in diminishing numbers. Once I saw a grey and ghostly battleship that may have been on a journey to be scrapped for its metal. I was not yet in residence for the Parade of Tall Ships from around the world that honored the 1976 Bicentennial, but I had my private viewing platform for the bigger procession of barques and brigantines that arrived to honor the Statue of Liberty's centennial a decade later.

I get a kick whenever I see the tide move "backwards" up the river, as it does twice a day for periods of more than six hours, propelling saltwater north from the ocean; if the wind is blowing inland, I can smell the salt. After an upstream run the river changes its course to run south for a similar amount of time. The more powerful downstream tide carries fresh water to the sea. And then the cycle is repeated in the Hudson's estuarial pattern. A solid knowledge of tides and currents is important for boat navigation; I am just an observer of surface flow.

Plenty of action takes place in the sky, and I find much of it unpleasant. My water feature lies midway in an air corridor for small planes and helicopters on various missions: escorting sightseers and financial-district commuters, advertising products, performing security surveillance for high-profile events. Officially called the Hudson River flyway, the air corridor is the fifteen-mile strip between the George Washington Bridge and the Verrazano Bridge, where the river passes through the Narrows to reach the ocean. For everyone's safety, small craft are directed to fly at altitudes below 1,300 feet while big jets command the sky at 30,000 feet and higher. Small-craft pilots are supposed to follow the "visual flight rules"—stay over the water, hew to a shoreline, keep your radio tuned to a frequency for traffic advisories. Travel time in one direction on the flyway is seven minutes if the pilot doesn't dawdle near The Lady. Once I saw a weekend warrior in a

'Knock Out' rose with Hudson River in background

biplane—weekend warriors are what these idiots are called—swerve inland to buzz a building for fun.

On Tuesday morning, September 11, 2001, I was sipping coffee and reading the paper when a friend called at 9 A.M.: "*Look out your window—I heard on the radio that a small plane crashed into the World Trade Center.*" That was how the news of terrorist hijackers was first reported. "*A small plane may have lost control. . . .*" I looked out my window, past my roses and the expanse of Greenwich Village, toward the twin towers, a looming presence vastly out of scale with the rest of the Lower Manhattan skyline. The top half of one tower was engulfed in flames. As I stared, unbelieving, a second jet dived into the other tower. *Oh my god!*

One tower collapsed at 10 A.M. The other fell a half-hour later. Everything was surreal, like Jean Cocteau's *The Blood of a Poet,* a silent black-and-white film with repeated images of a crumbling tower. The color TV in my bedroom kept replaying the footage of the crumbling twin towers. Sirens wailed as ambulances from Saint Vincent's Hospital sped downtown to collect the injured who might have survived. The president addressed the nation at 8:30 that evening. By then the air had become fetid with the dust of pulverized humans, and my apartment was filled with friends who were stranded and couldn't get home. Some of them slept over.

Sorry to have gone on about 9/11 in a garden book, but I could not suppress what I witnessed that day from my penthouse aerie near the Hudson River.

Sightseeing helicopters have become hugely profitable for entrepreneurs on both sides of the Hudson. I hear the noise from the engines and the whirring blades before the choppers come into view. The sound fills me with dread from another era: the whirring Huey gunships of the Vietnam War that I saw every night on the TV news. I am not the only person to hate the choppers. They are also big carbon dioxide polluters, and a few environmental groups and elected officials are calling for their outright ban. Good luck to them.

An infrequent but wondrous sight in winter, if we've had a spell of subfreezing weather, are the ice formations on the river's two shores that look as if they might meet in the middle, giving me sweet dreams of skating to New Jersey. The jagged floes never do converge. If they did, the Coast Guard ice patrol would break them up swiftly to keep the commercial traffic moving. On overcast, misty summer mornings the river presents another wondrous aspect: it becomes a long sheet of grey glass, a mirror that reflects the shape of the tall buildings on the opposite shore.

Fireworks pop up unexpectedly here and there on summer evenings, launched from a single barge for the enjoyment of invited guests on a nearby pleasure boat. Single-barge fireworks are paid for by folks that want to celebrate something—a wedding, an engagement, an anniversary, a birthday—with a big bang. The permit alone costs $50,000. Gay Pride Week in June used to end with fireworks from a barge that was right in front of me; the show started fashionably late at 10:20.

After all these years, I am pretty blasé about single-barge fireworks. That's because the best show of all for lighting up the sky is Macy's annual Fourth of July display that is often, but not always, fired from four synchronized barges between Chelsea and the mid-forties. When I moved to this penthouse, Macy's gift to the city turned me into a Fourth of July party giver, with all the attendant anxiety one has over hosting an outdoor event. Will it rain and be a washout? There were only two washouts in all the Fourths that Macy's and I have put on. The sweetest moment of the evening, in my opinion, comes after the grand finale, after the last whistle and boom of exploding chrysanthemums, peonies, rings, hearts, and palms (and the last *ooohs* and *ahhhs* from my guests) when hundreds of pleasure boats that gathered on the river to watch the show from their perspective begin their voyage home in the suddenly quiet dark.

I'm lucky to still see as much of the Hudson as I do. Every year a few more highrises spring up between the river and me on land that used to house factories and meatpacking plants outside the protection of the Greenwich Village Historic District. The city and some private interests have concocted grand plans for the derelict wood pilings that used to support working piers. Pier 52 was torn town for an amphitheater that will jut into the river. Pier 40, the site of a neighborhood soccer field, tennis courts, and dog runs, is up for grabs. The Whitney Museum built a new home on meatpacking district land in front of my eyes. After the cleverly designed structure opened to the public, I begrudgingly warmed to having an art museum close by and took out a membership *even though the damn thing blocked a chunk of my river view.*

It is an axiom of city life that people in tall buildings with astonishing but unprotected views will find their vistas obstructed by newer and taller buildings. Nobody owes me a sweeping view of the Hudson. One day, maybe in my lifetime, there won't be a river view from this terrace at all.

Quoting Ralph Waldo Emerson, circa 1846: "Who looks upon a river in a meditative hour and is not reminded of the flux of all things?"

BUSHELS OF PEACHES

B ob, the cheerful owner of the Canal Street garden center, marched me to the narrow south side of the terrace and pointed to a corner. "This spot cries out for a tree."

"Oh? There doesn't seem to be much room." Less than six feet on its hypotenuse side, the blunted triangle faced a bedroom window and one of the terrace doors. Bob's crew had already planted three birches on my western flank and lowered a balled-and-burlapped flowering crabapple into its home on the north side. I was a novice gardener suddenly rich in trees. Things arboreal were moving too fast. I felt overwhelmed.

"A grower sent me a dwarf peach. Says it's an Elberta."

Elberta was the magic word. To me, there is no better fruit in the world than a tangy, juicy, freestone Elberta in August. For peach growers and peach eaters, the Elberta is the standard by which all other peaches are judged. I can tell you now, because I've done some research, that the Elberta was bred and perfected on a Georgia plantation after the Civil War and named for the hybridizer's wife. I had never heard of a dwarf Elberta, but I could pull up from memory the sight of a full-size peach tree that dominated the backyard of a house in the Brooklyn neighborhood where I grew up. Kids and adults used to gather in the owner's driveway to stare at the miracle when it was bearing.

"Bob, would this dwarf really grow peaches? Full-size peaches?"

He shrugged. Bob never exaggerated. He knew the tree's success would depend on what kind of gardener I'd turn out to be. "Well," he said finally, "you'd have a good conversation piece."

I didn't need a conversation piece. But the thought, the anticipation, of biting into a slurpy peach that I had lovingly nurtured, a soft, luscious, yellow-fleshed peach dripping red juice, was irresistible.

A few days later, a crew from Bob's garden center brought over a scrawny little sapling and planted it in an angular box that fit snugly against the parapet. They secured the young specimen with guy wires for safety against the wind. The sapling did not look like it was up to the job of growing into a peach tree, but then again, I'd never seen a sapling before.

From my naive perspective, the peach tree did nothing much for its first two years, and I considered scrapping it. It didn't occur to me that its roots were digging in deep below the soil line and spreading, just as they were supposed to. Novice gardeners rarely consider what goes on below the surface, or understand its importance. Impatient for above-ground performance, I planted a dozen bulbs of the miniature daffodil 'Tete-a-Tete' around the base of the skinny trunk and jammed the fleshy roots of a clematis vine in a corner of the redwood box, doubtlessly causing confusion among these competing root systems. The little yellow daffs came up nicely for one season, nodding and waving at each other. 'General Sikorski', the clematis, sent up two strong vines that I tied to the wrought-iron railing. The clematis vines produced long buds that unfurled to reveal buff-colored stamens surrounded by large purple petals with faint red bars. The peach tree looked frail and sulky.

In its third spring, my peach tree flowered modestly. Following this feat, it burst out with a surprising number of shiny green elongated leaves that were unmistakably the foliage of a peach tree. Late in the summer, the tree produced six fantastically large, juicy peaches. Real freestone Elbertas. My miracle had begun. I started reading everything I could find about peaches. Rare among fruit trees, a peach does not require a mate for pollination, as do apples and pears. A self-fruitful tree is ideal for limited space, and a dwarf tree is perfect. I sent for a free report on peach growing from Cornell's agricultural extension service and learned that peach trees do best on a south-facing slope. Exactly the conditions I had, sort of. Then I turned the pages of the report and read about "June drop," which solved, at least intellectually, a new mystery I had encountered.

June drop is survival of the fittest in the world of fruit trees. A peach tree will produce far more immature peaches than it can bring to fruition, so in June a large number of hard nugget-size green peaches will give up the ghost and fall to the ground, enabling the rest of the crop to mature. Obviously, "fall to the ground" is wildly different on a high Manhattan terrace than it would be in a peach orchard. Some of my tree's hard green nuggets bounced twenty floors to the street. A percentage of the June drop plopped onto the terrace of the neighbor below me. I thought about netting the tree during the annual crisis of June drop, but the idea seemed impractical and ugly. In a beautification measure I removed the guy wires that lashed the tree to the wrought-iron railing. The tree was on its own, and my reputation for being an inconsiderate neighbor was growing.

In its heyday, my bountiful tree produced more than a bushel of peaches every summer. The fruit was absolutely delicious—authentic Elberta—though its red skin was a trifle thick, a protective response to what the peaches had endured in the wind. On rare occasions I discovered a tiny puncture wound on a peach—perhaps a bird had taken a peck and found that peach flavor was not to its liking.

My hugely serious problem was tactical. All the peaches ripened and needed to be picked during one frantic week in August. I acquired a professional fruit-picking pole and became adept at the twist of the wrist that snares a peach and draws it down safely. I'd invite friends to drop by for my annual harvesting party. I gave away baskets of peaches to the building's staff. I made peach pie and peach ice cream. I found a recipe for peach chutney with raisins, ginger, and mustard seeds in

The author with her roses and peach tree (*right*)

a book on preserving. My recipe for peach jam came from a very precise book by the French dessert chef Lenôtre. Briefly, macerate peaches in sugar overnight; drain and boil syrup the following morning; add peaches and vanilla bean; boil for ten minutes; stir in lemon juice; remove immediately from heat and fill sterilized jars. For one crazed week every August I was skinning, pitting, and macerating peaches in bowls all over the dining room, stirring pots on the kitchen stove with a wooden spoon, and bottling up the product in cute little mason jars.

At this juncture in my absorbing life with peaches, my dwarf's slender grey limbs and elongated green leaves had reached the rooftop. Fruit on the highest boughs was easy picking for the building's staff. I thought it was only fair when a porter leaned over the roof to grab a peach, but the tree's insistent upward and outward growth was alarming. Heavily laden branches hung way over the terrace and exceeded the reach of my picking pole, even when I climbed into the planter box with the pole and leaned over as far as I could to execute the twist-and-catch maneuver. After one too-bountiful harvest I purchased a Japanese crosscut pruning saw, and executed some major cuts on the tree's loftiest branches. Perhaps I should have made more.

I have to confess that while I was hauling in my annual crop, sometimes a ripe peach accidentally fell. Usually it smashed onto my territory, but there were occasions when it plunged two flights down to a neighbor's terrace.

"They're animals up there," the downstairs neighbor complained to another downstairs neighbor. "They take one bite out of a peach and throw it over the railing."

The remark got passed back to me. In my arrogance I believed the downstairs neighbor should have understood that ripe fruit can fall from a tree, and that I was doing my best to snatch every peach before it fell of its own accord. My righteous insensitivity in those days appalls me. I was harvesting homegrown peaches while my downstairs neighbor got splatter. It would have been so simple to give her a basket of peaches or a jar of jam as a way to make amends. I never did. In retrospect, I realize that neighbor was a very good sport. She never kicked up a fuss with the building's management, unlike the crank nine floors below me on the north side. He had his lawyer write me threatening "cease and desist" letters about the petals that wafted down to the crank's terrace from my flowering crabapple.

One winter, maybe fifteen years into my miraculous harvest, we had an extreme cold spell. There were dire predictions in the news about how the prolonged sub-zero weather would affect the summer crop of New Jersey peaches. New Jersey's big orchards and I were in this peril together. When spring came, a few pinched blossoms appeared on my tree's branches and withered. The tree failed to leaf out. My peach tree had died.

The crop of New Jersey Elbertas was small and tasteless that year. In my own private hell, I had the sad task of using my elegant Japanese saw to cut down my dead tree's branches. I did the job in manageable stages, sawing large limbs into smaller pieces, and then carrying the pathetic bundles to the compactor room down the hall. Uprooting the trunk and getting the huge mass out of the redwood box required more strength than I possessed. I paid one of the building's porters to execute that final chore.

A butterfly bush in a polyurethane tub now occupies the corner where once I had a conversation piece and bushels of peaches.

A FIELD OF COREOPSIS

This story has a happy ending, so bear with me. For three decades I had a field of golden coreopsis. Well, it wasn't truly a field, it was a row of *Coreopsis verticillata* 'Zagreb' in five tongue-and-groove redwood boxes on the western perimeter of the terrace. If I stood at one end and gazed down the row, which I did quite often, I had the illusion of a vast flowering field that waved and danced at the Hudson River shoreline.

Creating an illusion of a greater expanse in a small-space garden is an excellent project. Some people use a strategically placed mirror or paint a *trompe l'oeil* gate on a wall. My idea for a coreopsis field came after I'd enjoyed one season of mixed annuals in the narrow boxes. The short zinnias, dahlias, and marigolds interspersed with alyssum looked terrific but left me hankering for a permanent planting. In those days I wanted nothing but permanent plantings. Raves in the Wayside Gardens catalog for coreopsis, "a tireless performer" and "the plant with a sunny disposition," inspired me to try this daisy-lookalike with a horticultural moniker I'd never heard of.

Coreopsis never failed me. It's a common perennial, an American native, and a roadside grower that seldom fails anyone. New hybrids regularly appear in the catalogs, but the golden 'Zagreb' is the one I know and love. I wish I knew why it shares its name with the capital of Croatia, but I haven't yet found any clues on the Web. An individual coreopsis flower is nothing to get excited about—eight petals of a modest size surround a small tuft on a wiry stem. *Verticillata* foliage is called "threadleaf," but I'd call it fernlike or ferny. The plants spread via rhizomes—horizontal stems below the soil line—that send up new shoots like a fireworks display. The coreopsis blooming period runs through the entire summer if I pluck off the spent flowers and cut back the foliage to a triangular joint.

My faux field was a great hit with my friends. "Do you know," they'd say, "if you stand over here you get the impression that the daisies are growing at the river's edge."

"Yes I know," I'd answer proudly. "Coreopsis is a humble plant, but for me it creates magic."

My struggle with coreopsis came every spring, when the new ferny growth emerged and it was time to wrench out the dead stalks I'd let winter over. This chore required garden gloves, multiple trash bags, and considerable stooping. Sometimes I'd sit; sometimes I'd kneel. Usually I executed the job in short, strenuous bursts over a three-day period, muttering and cursing as I wrenched and bagged. Repetitive labor is an unavoidable duty for everyone with a garden, except for those who rely on hired help. Some chores on the terrace are beyond my physical strength and I gladly paid others to do the work, but the repetitive chore of wrenching out dead stalks, along with planting, weeding, watering, pruning, and replenishing the soil, is my job, or I could not call myself a gardener.

And now the sad part. One day in high season I lost the five redwood planters and their lovingly nurtured contents in a terrible misunderstanding between John the superintendent and an "architectural engineer" the management hired who was neither an architect nor an engineer and who shall go nameless here. The tongue-and-groove boxes, in perfect condition and brimming with flowers, were demolished to comply with New York's Local Law 11 regarding potential leaks, a law that few people understand but everyone must comply with. My table and chairs were also demolished in the confusion. People with terrace gardens, renters or owners, have no right of redress, no appeals court, when orders come down from management

'Zagreb'

about Local Law 11. Powerless to stop the destruction, I salvaged one coreopsis rhizome and replanted it in a small pot. The following spring I dragged my potted daylily collection to the site of my former field.

Beautiful as daylilies are, their blooming period is short and staggered, and mismatched pots do not create the illusion of a field. A single coreopsis plant in a pot isn't much of a statement, either. John the superintendent tried to make amends for my loss by giving me a table that a second-floor patio owner wished to discard, but my grief could not be assuaged by furniture. One inconsolable year later, I recommitted to coreopsis.

All it took (gulp!) was $2,000, a bigger bite out of my yearly income than it had been three decades earlier. Technology had changed and wood was passé. From plantcontainers.com I ordered five polyurethane troughs that were textured and tinted to resemble weathered clay, with predrilled holes, and filled them with twenty bags of soil delivered from Barney's Hardware, a neighborhood institution. Then I scoured the catalogs, in print and online, to choose my replacement coreopsis. After mulling over the fringed, fluted, pink, orange, and white varieties, the new and improved this and that with maroon eyes and burgundy splashes, I found my old friend 'Zagreb' at santarosagardens.com and ordered fifteen starters. One cloudy spring morning I planted them ecstatically, assigning three ferny clumps to each "weathered clay" station.

The first year's growth was disappointing, as is generally the case with perennials that need more time than annuals to establish themselves underground. A paltry number of pinpoint buds and undersized flowers made me leap to the conclusion that something had gone wrong. By their second spring the rhizomes had done their job of spreading below the soil line and were sending up green starbursts beyond their mother plants to the containers' edges. I resumed my old task of twisting off the previous year's dead stalks, working my ungloved fingers gently to protect the tender new growth from being uprooted by a thoughtless yank. As I isolated and pulled each stalk I crooned something tuneless: "Eyes, fingers, thumb joint . . . Eyes, fingers, thumb joint." The monotonous chant and the tactile intimacy of twisting and pulling kept me focused during the long task.

Now it's up to 'Zagreb' to continue spreading, to faultlessly produce an abundance of ferny leaves and bright golden flowers every summer, and become a magical field again.

Note: Change your body posture frequently during your spring bout with coreopsis. Take a break from the chore by stretching or lying down, as you might at the gym after an exercise class. Do not forget to water! Your plants are exhausted, as you are, by your sudden attack on their contained world. They will perk up quickly after a deep watering.

Note one year later: 'Zagreb' is still struggling to become a golden field. During its hiatus I'd forgotten that the original planting took a few years to fill out its containers, and that bumblebees like coreopsis as much as I do. I'd forgotten the bees' kamikaze dives into the flower tufts, their infernal suck-suck-sucking to extract nectar and pollen—*an act of aggression that destroys the flowers.* I'd forgotten the bees' sense of entitlement, and my vigilant patrols to pinch off the petals' shriveled remains.

Bees prefer to alight on large swaths of blooms where they can find lots of food in one place, and coreopsis ranks high on the list of flowers that bees like to feast on. Only in whispers is it mentioned that bees can decimate 60 percent of a flower crop in their insatiable quest. My golden field is their golden field. I swat them; they flinch and come back. I spray the field's perimeter with a smelly insecticide; the bees look annoyed, dart away, and return. At some point, perhaps when they've reached their 60 percent quota (just kidding), they move on to my penstemon, my campanula, and return to my butterfly bush, their favorite location. "Where the bees suck, there swat I." Sorry, Shakespeare and Ariel.

Note three years later: My attempt to re-create my original coreopsis field ran into two difficulties. First off, I'd misjudged the height of the "weathered clay" rectangular planters. They are one foot shorter than my original wood boxes, which means that the coreopsis blooms barely reach the parapet's wrought-iron railing. A difference of one foot in height is not the main reason why the new row of coreopsis does not present the illusion that the flowers are dancing at the river's edge. The main reason is the construction of tall buildings on the land between the river and me. There is nothing I can do about that.

The second unexpected happenstance was the horrendously cold winter and non-spring of 2014–2015 that decimated my roses, my favorite hydrangea, and most of the rhizomes in one of the coreopsis troughs. I don't know why one trough was cursed and not the others, but that is what happened. I went on a frantic search for replacements—'Zagreb' is no longer a popular variety among coreopsis fanciers—and discovered that eBay merchants sell all kinds of seedlings, including, miraculously, my dear old friend 'Zagreb'. The deal on eBay was $18.99 for ten seedlings with free shipping, a very reasonable price. The seedlings arrived lickety-split from New Jersey wrapped in wet newspaper inside a Kleenex box with a full page of intimidating instructions that boiled down to "Plant in the evening and keep well watered." A few seedlings were too scrawny to bother with, but I received more than enough good ones for my purpose, and they worked out just fine.

EXPERIMENTAL STATIONS

What I keep or don't keep on my terrace is about what thrills me or leaves me cold and about what I thought should do well but doesn't. After years of decent growth, I ditched a row of black-eyed Susans because they seemed out of place in an urban setting. Scabiosa was boring. Purple loosestrife, a known invasive, did not establish a beachhead here. Blue *Caryopteris* was a magnet for beetles. I acidified the soil as recommended for astilbe and heather, but they didn't make it. Swamp mallow? What was I thinking? When I started my garden I didn't mind the losses. I worried that I'd run out of space. Between the quitters, the ill-fitters, and the successes undone by the building's periodic renovations, I've always had room for something new.

Fruits and vegetables needed more growing room than I suspected; I learned the hard way. Some flowering plants send up vast amounts of spreading foliage before they deign to show their pretty faces. Black plastic bags for growing lettuce were chiefly collectors of terrace debris. For one full growing season I admired the tropical-looking foliage of the rhubarb 'Valentine' and refrained from pulling any stalks in order to strengthen the plant as it settled in, yet for all my forbearance 'Valentine' did not come back for a second year. Neither did my gooseberry bush. My carrots were two-pronged and hairy, giving me a profound respect for carrot farmers and "fine tilth." Beets needed greater depth for their taproots than I'd imagined. My tomatoes, bought in gallon cans at local markets, gave me a fright with hornworms and whitefly. The dormant blueberry bushes I ordered were so huge when they arrived that I did not even bother to take them out of the box. I pestered a fellow on

Goldenrod

Long Island who sold pear trees on espalier frames, but he had the good sense to turn me down.

I used to avoid spring-blooming perennials, except for my adored peony bush, because I wanted color all over the place from spring to fall, but now I am willing to go for fleeting joy in experimental stations, a few sixteen- and eighteen-inch pots I keep around for what strikes my fancy. If I hadn't relaxed my rules on ephemeral bloomers I'd have missed the chance to witness the growth habits of many celebrated beauties.

Poppies, of which there are many kinds, bring up diverse associations: evanescent beauty, opium traffic, poppyseed cakes, remembering the war dead in Flanders Field. I wanted a poppy experience. One fall day I planted a single specimen of *Papaver orientalis* 'Burning Heart' acquired from Jung in Wisconsin. Oriental poppies are native to the

Caucasus, northern Iran, and Turkey. "Oriental" is an overly broad, antiquated word that most people find offensive nowadays when it is used to describe a person, but it's still okay for a flower.

In its first spring 'Burning Heart' sent up one large bud atop low, serrated foliage. I hovered over the bud, measured the stem, poked into the foliage, and determined that at this early stage of what I hoped would be a long life, the plant was going to bear only one flower. My poppy opened over the Memorial Day weekend, a fitting time for poppies and for remembering the graves of soldiers. Tissue-paper petals, a watercolor wash of pink with black blotches, framed a dark, shiny center of seeds and stamens. 'Burning Heart' was ravishing—I took its picture from several angles and posted the best one on Facebook. On its third day, the flower withered in unseasonable heat. Soon after, the leaves went dormant, as oriental poppies are wont to do. When Memorial Day rolled around the following year, 'Burning Heart' had plenty of poppy foliage and no poppy flowers. That became its yearly story; my patience wore thin and eventually I scuttled it.

Good news! Goldenrod, that maligned roadside grower, has been exonerated of all charges that it is a late-summer scourge for hay fever sufferers; its pollen is too heavy to go airborne and the service of a bee or a butterfly is required for reproduction. Ragweed is hay fever's culprit, an ugly sneak that grows unnoticed near goldenrod patches and wafts its pollen into sinuses for miles around. More good news! *Solidago* 'Little Lemon', a dwarf goldenrod eighteen inches tall including its spikey flowerheads, is perfect for containers on a high city terrace. 'Little Lemon' was hybridized in Israel, a very small country with a thriving horticulture industry that developed a subspecialty in downsizing big plants.

'Little Lemon' has been with me for five years, so it is past the experiment stage. Like its tall roadside relatives, it is perfectly hardy and does best in full sun. Early in summer tiny green dots of flower

Hollyhock

buds emerge in tight clusters at the top of its slender-leafed stems. By late July the clusters mature into short plumes the color of lemon rind that adorn the plant through August. Not such good news: One year tiny hoverflies drew nectar from my goldenrod's flowers, draining the plumes of their color. Pollinators never quit searching for new opportunities. There are many kinds of hoverflies (some mimic wasps and bees); I hear they are beneficial insects in the country, but they are not beneficial to me.

Here is a rave for *Campanula carpatica* 'Blue Clips', a short, mounding perennial with upturned violet bells that bloom tirelessly from summer to fall. When my garden was new, I tucked a circle of 'Blue Clips' into the birch tree tubs. The plants were so charming that I finally put three 'Blue Clips' in their own rectangular trough, a wise decision since soon enough the birches' roots needed every bit of space in their tubs for themselves. As with so many plants on my terrace, I'd never seen a campanula before I started growing them. Tall campanulas do not hold up to the wind, but the little *carpatica* is only eight inches high and one foot wide; it is not its fault that bees love to guzzle at its trough. The *carpatica* species is native to the Carpathian Mountains of Eastern Europe, which explains its rugged disposition. Hares that nibble on campanulas may have led to their alternative name of hare-bell, or at least I like to think so.

The balloon flower, *Platycodon grandiflorus,* is an Asian member of the campanula family that has flower buds resembling hot-air balloons before they unfold their starry petals. Years ago I bought two balloon flower plants from the Bluestone catalog, one purple and one white, neither exceeding one-and-a-half feet in height. The clump with the white balloon flowers is still with me, neatly contained in a fourteen-inch pot where it sends up its fun balloons all summer; the purple balloon flower did not come back for a second year. Why, I don't know. Maybe its pot got waterlogged over the winter. Anyway, I mean to try another purple balloon flower because it's a dandy plant, and I never tire of the color purple in my garden.

To my surprise, junior-size hollyhocks less than three feet tall began appearing in the catalogs in the spring of 2013—I'd been pining for a small hollyhock since I'd started my terrace garden. The first dwarf *Alcea* I planted, a frilly pink-and-white that I placed near the divider

Poppy

between my terrace and a neighbor's, sent up vigorous stalks, flowers, and seedpods for the entire summer. Initially I mistook the seedpods for new flower buds and even tied a laden stalk to the railing. Then I began to understand that the hollyhock's mission is to broadcast seeds all over the place, which may be a desirable trait in a barnyard but not on a small urban terrace where they will root between the pavers and unwanted hollyhock seedlings will pop up all over the place the following spring. The trick is to cut a stalk down to its basal growth as soon as the dread seedpods appear.

Hollyhocks are biennials, which means one year to grow from seed and a second year to flower, then to die. I buy a second-year plant in the spring, always on the lookout for a new color. In the fall I wrench it out and throw it away. The apricot shade was lovely but it faded to white in the sun. This year I've got a vivid crimson. The color range of these dwarfs is still limited, but probably won't be for long.

I'd never heard of penstemon until the playwright Lanford Wilson told me it was his favorite flower and that he grew many kinds at his vacation house in the Hamptons. In his play *The Fifth of July* a married couple obsess about buying gravel for their penstemon bed—Wilson knew that some penstemons flourish in gravel! So, inspired by a playwright whose work I admired, I began searching the mail-order catalogs for a penstemon that would be right for a city terrace, but the available species were too large. Twenty years after we'd had our conversation, a short hybrid named 'Mexicali Red Rocks' appeared in the Bluestone catalog—finally a penstemon that was right for me.

Penstemon (pronounced PEN-stemon) in the wild is a short-lived flowering perennial found on arid, sunny plains and in dry, rocky mountainous regions from Canada to Guatemala, often at elevations above ten thousand feet. Its numerous species vary in size and habit from one-inch mat-forming alpines to eight-foot giants. 'Mexicali Red Rocks', a cross between a Mexican and an American strain, is eighteen inches tall and bears small, bright cerise bells with cerise-and-white striped throats. 'Red Rocks' blooms lavishly through the summer and fall if I cut back the stems after they've flowered. Bluestone called it a magnet for butterflies, but for me it is a magnet for bees; the intruders snuggle into the small, charming bells after they feast on my coreopsis and assault my campanula. I wonder if the white stripes inside the bells are a landing guide for the bees. Does everything in nature have a purpose?

Buoyed by the success of 'Red Rocks' I devoted a second pot on the terrace to the slightly taller, more upright 'Pikes Peak Purple', a violet mexicali with a white-and-violet striped throat. Both penstemons were hybridized by Bruce Meyers in his hometown of White Salmon, Washington. Meyers, who rose to become a president of the American

Penstemon Society, was an artist who was felling trees for a living when he started making his ingenious crosses.

The two Meyers hybrids I grow were named for the spectacular red granite formations of the Colorado Rocky Mountains, part of the American frontier once called "the Kansas Territory" that was populated by nomadic Utes who believed the majestic peak towering over their hunting grounds was the site of the creation. The Utes called the peak "Sun Mountain Sitting Big," but it became "Pike's Peak" to honor Zebulon Pike, a surveyor for the U.S. Army. Gold seekers rolling across the prairies in the late 1850s put the jaunty sign "Pike's Peak or Bust" on their covered wagons; the apostrophe was eventually abandoned, as were most of the gold-seekers' dreams.

If you don't mind their brief lives—three years max for me— mexicali penstemons are a good choice for a high, sunny, and windy urban terrace. All penstemons are drought resistant and require little water, though a potted penstemon in a breezy habitat like mine needs regular watering and a shot of Miracle-Gro now and then. I'm smiling as I mention Miracle-Gro. Some of today's penstemon hybridizers shudder at the idea of applying a chemical fertilizer to their plants. Natural sustainable gardening is their evangelistic mission, while my mission is simply to sustain what I'm growing.

I've got my eye on the deep garnet mexicali 'Windwalker' that was bred in Colorado for greenhouse wholesalers and hasn't yet been released to the mail-order hordes. Ditto for the pink-and-white mexicali 'Carolyn's Hope'. Its Colorado hybridizer donates all proceeds from sales to breast cancer research. You can see him among his rows of 'Carolyn's Hope' on YouTube if you wish. I'm also nursing along a penstemon seedling on my windowsill that took root between the pavers near its mother plant. Penstemons from seed don't always breed true, so who knows what will come from this adventure.

Lavender is an aromatic shrub with a long history of medicinal claims, like calming the nerves, that is grown commercially and most famously in the dazzling fields of Provence in southern France for its essential oils that infuse soaps and perfumes. Pleasure gardeners grow lavender for its beauty.

On impulse late one summer when I suddenly needed to fill a trough on the north side of my terrace, I picked up three pots of Lavender 'Grosso' at the Union Square market. Lavender 'Grosso' was discovered in 1972 by a French farmer named Grosso who noticed the accidental hybrid was outperforming his other lavender shrubs. It had a remarkable rate of return and a very long blooming season, thanks to a genetic mix that combined the cold-hardiness of English lavender with the tolerance for heat of a Portuguese species. 'Grosso' is one of the world's most popular lavenders today. Do you think I knew any of this when I bought my three pots? I didn't.

I crowded my trio of lavenders cheek-to-jowl into their designated trough. They bloomed sparsely for the rest of the season as they stretched toward the afternoon sun. Lavender had never honored me by returning for a second season wherever I'd planted it, even in full sun where lavender does best. I considered this trough a one-season show.

The following spring a multitude of flower wands floated above the gray-green foliage that had wakened from its winter rest. When the graceful wands began to show their emblematic lavender color, the trough was picture-perfect.

A single trough of lavender is not as breathtaking as the lavender fields of Provence or the swaths of lavender bathed in full sun along the Hudson River Park, where I sometimes take a walk, but my lavender trough is up-close and personal and exactly the right size for my terrace. Perhaps down the line I might have to dig out two of the 'Grosso' shrubs to allow the one in the center to expand to a normal size. Perhaps not. Perhaps these lavenders will be happy dwarfs. I'll take my cue from the lavenders.

COMING UP ROSES

Roses are great for a high city terrace if you choose the right rose. The right rose is not one of the long-stemmed beauties that are flown in daily from Ecuador and Colombia where work in the flower fields is low-paid and grueling. Also unsuitable are tall grandifloras, finicky hybrid teas, huge arching ramblers, and the magnificent heritage roses obsessively collected by the Empress Josephine at Malmaison that were painted by Redouté and not intended for windy conditions. The right rose is a repeat-blooming shrub about three feet in height and width that might have a strain of the wild *rugosa* species in its DNA. A hardy climber can work, if you have an available south wall and a tall ladder.

I'm not revealing a secret here, but it must be said that roses have thorns that viciously prick your skin and draw blood when you are pruning the rose for its own good and welfare. In these unpleasant encounters you are foolishly working without gloves, or even more foolish, with bare arms. Perhaps you are wearing a knitted sweater, which to a rose is reckless attire just begging to get snagged. Maybe you think you are admirably prepared for your pruning session because your armor consists of long sleeves and puncture-proof gloves—and your rose punctures the inch of exposed skin on your wrists between your gloves and sleeves. Marianne Moore's witty poem "Roses Only" concludes, "Your thorns are the best part of you." Moore was probably addressing a prickly friend, not a real rose, or perhaps she was describing herself.

The ancestral diversity of the rose is so complex that I pity the rose historians who try to make sense of it. In short, the genus *Rosa* seems to have originated in China and Persia and spread to Europe and nearly everywhere else through hybridizing and cultivation, and by the rose's own genetic imperative to defend itself and conquer new territory. The rose survives not only because it gives us so much beauty and fragrance—it provides an essential oil for making perfumes, it produces seed hips rich in Vitamin C and pectin that we use to make teas, jams, and jellies, and that birds feast on and disperse through their droppings. The rose's evolutionary adaptation of thorns is one of the flower world's greatest deterrents against browsing animals and grabby humans. Elsewhere I've said that new growth is tender, but I exclude the rose from that observation. A newly emerging rose cane looks ready to win any battle.

My journey with roses has taken me on a long path. Some beloved favorites recommended by the catalogs lasted only one season. An arching rambler was more vigorous than I expected, although the catalog did mention a fifteen-foot spread. I learned that lax canes handle themselves better in wind than rigid upright canes, which look awkward in a container anyway. I reconciled myself to the practical fact that I could not grow a big, blowsy cabbage rose that represents my idea of a British cottage garden. Roses that tolerate urban terrace conditions have flowers that rarely exceed two and a half inches, but they bloom in clusters, so the effect is almost as splendid. Well, the effect is sufficient. I still yearn for a voluptuous, swirly, iced cupcake of a rose that won't be shredded to pieces by the wind, but that precious hybrid hasn't yet been invented.

I grow, and am grateful to, some popular modern hybrids that are sent to market bearing descriptions like "carefree" and "tireless performer" but never "fragrant." If one quality must be sacrificed to make a rose carefree and tireless, I don't mind the loss of fragrance since my sense of smell is so poor. Once a Korean grocer, new to the neighborhood, shyly asked me if people were rushing to buy his lilacs

'William Baffin'

'Bonica'

because they smelled so good, and I blithely assured him that lilacs had no fragrance. Standing amid his pails of lilacs, he was too polite to disagree.

The oldest rose on my terrace, in terms of its decades of service to me, is 'The Fairy', a scentless two-foot—sometimes taller—pink polyantha that bears tiny pompons in profuse clusters and is said to be the most popular rose in the world. 'The Fairy' was introduced in 1932 by the British rose breeder Ann Bentall. Ann and her husband John were staff gardeners for the eminent rosarian Joseph Pemberton, who ceded them acreage and greenhouses in his will. Some of Ann

Bentall's roses are still widely cultivated, yet they bore the Pemberton imprimatur for a half-century before she was rightfully credited.

In its rosy bud stage, 'The Fairy' reminds me of those classic Liberty of London patterns that look so sweet on a cotton blouse. Left to its own devices, it spreads into a thicket that must be rigorously pruned, or it will fall prey to mildew on its lower branches in its tireless habit of sending up new shoots and buds. I usually remember to wear long rubber gloves when I'm pruning 'The Fairy'—its infuriating capacity to snag bare skin belies the eponymous children's book fairy with gossamer wings. 'The Fairy' moves into action later than my other roses

61

(ah, the anticipation!). I have to admit that its clustered blooms fade to white in strong sun. There's nothing I can do about that. 'The Fairy' isn't a grand rose; it's a twinkle-toes workhorse and I love it. Among its many plusses, 'The Fairy' does not attract bees.

I've worked with several other polyanthas that were low-growing and charming. 'Little White Pet' was a winner for many years until it gave up after an extremely cold winter and I didn't replace it because I decided that red and pink roses were what I liked best. 'Nathalie Nypels' may have a short natural life span (I've lost it twice), but I find this Dutch hybrid to be the essence of charm.

I avoided 'Bonica' when it was introduced in the 1980s by Meilland, a family company in the south of France with strong international connections; I felt the new shrub was getting entirely too much publicity as the harbinger of a new race of roses. I was being pigheaded. Three feet and spreading into a shapely mound, 'Bonica' is used for highway meridians because of its hardiness and disease resistance. I've stationed it in the southwest corner of my terrace, where a birch tree once rocked in the wind. 'Bonica' is too low to rock its tub, and I can see the bush in all its glory from my bedroom window. Loosely cupped flowers froth in clusters, appearing more delicate than they are, with coloring that defies an easy description. I'd say bubblegum pink paling to white on the outer petals. Does that explain it? I get nostalgic for Fleer's Dubble Bubble, the bubblegum of my childhood, when I look at 'Bonica'. In the fall it bears orange hips for a bonus. 'Bonica' does not attract bees, either.

When the disease-resistant 'Knock Out' series created by Bill Radler of Wisconsin began making news, I acted more swiftly than I did with 'Bonica'. For the terrace's northwest corner that once held a birch, I chose Radler's original 'Knock Out', a semi-double red with leaves that emerge in burgundy tones before they turn green. YouTube has a clip of Radler biting into a rose hip in a field of 'Knock Outs'; he looks as if he'd rather be in his experimental greenhouses making his crosses.

After I started tending his first 'Knock Out', Radler's grower and distributor Conard-Pyle released a whole series of 'Knock Outs' in a spectrum of colors. The new ones may be better than the original, but I didn't have room for a second Radler hybrid, and the one I had did not make me love it. As promised, the rose was totally disease resistant, and it stayed in bloom until late fall as my last rose of summer, but in five years the shrub did not fully command its tub, its foliage suffered from wind damage, and its canes veered away from northerly blasts. The deal breaker was that I disliked the electric neon glow of its red flowers.

In 2014 I made firm plans to replace the 'Knock Out' with 'Fire Meidiland', a spreading two-footer with clustered, double dark-red blooms from Meilland, the French company that won my respect with 'Bonica'. (Conard-Pyle grows and distributes 'Fire Meidiland' in America.) 'Fire Meidiland' arrived in a long box in early spring, its canes bristling with buds, but Radler's 'Knock Out' had already leafed out, and I lost my resolve to trash it. The act seemed cruel, and what did I really know about 'Fire Meidiland' beyond a pretty picture and its reported popularity on the West Coast for erosion control? In a sort of contest I planted 'Fire Meidiland' near the 'Knock Out' in a low tub that I knew was too small for its spreading habits and waited to see which rose I'd prefer. To my joy, there wasn't a trace of electric neon in the newcomer's small, velvety, dark red flowers.

For three low rectangular planters that I see from my south-facing living room windows, I initially went with 'Feisty', a ballyhooed new introduction, because its modest size seemed perfect. I made a mistake. The planters are molded grey polyurethane that mimics weathered granite with a bas-relief of acanthus leaves on their corners.

'Nathalie Nypels'

'Feisty' threw up flowers that were blood red with yellow stamens; in combination with the planters, the effect looked like a tribute to a Mafia boss at a New Jersey funeral parlor. Worse, 'Feisty' stunned me in its second year by coming down with a bad case of blackspot, the first time I had to deal with this deadly destroyer of foliage. What is feisty about a rose that succumbs to blackspot?

I dug out 'Feisty', replaced the soil, and put in 'Nathalie Nypels', a cupped semi-double polyantha in subtle shades of pink with glossy green foliage that I ordered online from the Antique Rose Emporium in Texas. Its full name is 'Mevrouw Nathalie Nypels' (Mevrouw is "Mrs." in English), and it was introduced in 1919 by the Dutch breeder Leenders. At two and a half feet tall, its habits are charming, it doesn't succumb to blackspot, its thorns aren't vicious, it repeats during the summer, and does not attract bees. My beautiful row of 'Nathalie Nypels' faces the Lower Manhattan skyline in the distance. Delightful.

I don't know why so few American gardeners grow this rose. If it succeeds with me, it should succeed for anyone with a sunny garden in a temperate climate.

I am thrilled with the Canadian climber 'William Baffin' that I grow against a brick wall that faces south. Before I describe it, I have to pause and take a deep breath, because one never forgets one's first love. 'New Dawn' was my first love. 'New Dawn' has a famous history in the plant world; its history with me was tragic. A vigorous grower with twenty-foot canes and clusters of double blush-pink blooms that repeat during the summer and fall, 'New Dawn' is a sport, or mutation, of 'Dr. W. Van Fleet', which flowers only in the spring. The happy accident was discovered in a rose nursery in 1930; the following year it became the first patented rose in commercial distribution. As a matter of fact, 'New Dawn' was the first patented plant material of any kind. Nowadays, patented seeds, genetically modified soybean seeds in particular, are a big boon to agribusiness but not to small farmers. I see that if I continue in this vein I'll be wandering far off the subject of roses. Anyway, the patent on 'New Dawn' has expired, so if you want to graft and sell one, please do.

'New Dawn' was a serious challenge. A climbing rose must be supported by a trellis or with special hooked nails that are hammered into the wall at intervals. I chose to hammer in the hooked nails and to tie the canes to the nails with plastic strips for extra security. As 'New Dawn' spread horizontally and vertically to the edge of the building's rooftop above me, I bought more packets of nails and more rolls of plastic ties, a tall ladder, and a battery-operated drill, but a year never went by without windstorms undoing some of my work. I had to call on the building's porters for their assistance. This was before the co-op turned the roof into a roof garden, so all the guys needed to do in those days was to hang over the railing and retie the canes of 'New Dawn' to their anchors. I paid them handsomely for their emergency aid and I like to think they were glad to help because 'New Dawn' in bloom was a commanding presence that could be seen from several streets away if someone looked up at my terrace, as I frequently did.

'New Dawn' came to a brutal end when the building went through one of its pointing and rebricking operations; this one, as I recall, was to stabilize the rooftop parapet above me. I will skip lightly over this terrible misfortune and how my love was carted away in pieces. Recovering from the blow and faced with an empty wall, I pinned my hopes on 'Zepherine Drouhin', an elegant Bourbon that graces the walls of the best European gardens, but it did not take to the accommodations I offered.

The hardy 'William Baffin', introduced in 1983, had no trouble adjusting. Named for a British explorer of the Canadian wilderness, it is short for a climber, so I can handle it by myself. Canada's Explorer Series, a thirty-year hybridizing program that extended the range of high-quality roses to that country's cold and harsh north, was government funded—imagine that! Felicitas Svejda, the series developer, was a plant geneticist who was born and trained in Austria. Her creations have migrated in turn to the coldest climate zones in the United States and Europe. 'William Baffin' puts on a glorious show in the spring, blanketing its south wall in clusters of deep pink, lightly scented roses that open to reveal pale yellow stamens. Bees are inordinately fond of 'Baffin'; I wish they weren't. Although many growers insist it repeats later in the season, 'William Baffin' does not repeat for me, and its orange hips are sparse and insignificant. What the rose does frequently, in the manner of climbers, is to shoot horizontal canes away from the wall that are too strong to bend back and tie in. I should mention that the paved walkway between 'Baffin''s wall and the outer railing of my terrace is very narrow. Even though 'Baffin' has relatively few thorns, it is a nuisance to brush past the outlying canes. I wait until they are full of rosy buds, and then cut them off for a week's display in an indoor vase. It took me years to hit upon this strategy.

In 2014–2015, the Northeast suffered its coldest, iciest winter in sixty-five years. Snowstorm followed snowstorm, with bouts of freezing rain in between. The sun deserted us. Howling winds toppled normally sure-footed pedestrians who sprawled into drifts of icy snow. I went about my business with caution and did not give any thought to my roses. Spring, such as it was, arrived in the middle of May with a hot spell that we usually don't get until midsummer. When I ventured onto the terrace, I saw that 'William Baffin' was the only rose to leaf out, although the long canes of 'Fire Meidiland' eventually greened up in its too-small tub. All my other roses were dead or dying. 'Bonica' and the 'Knock Out', in my two most exposed stations, showed no signs of life whatsoever. 'The Fairy' and the three 'Nathalie Nypels' looked like one-armed bandits in a Vegas casino—one green cane standing amid brown and shriveled dead wood.

My major plant losses over the years had been caused by human-induced catastrophes, chiefly rebricking and pointing. The year 2015 was a natural disaster. After an anguished period of mourning I did what I had to do—I began to scour the online catalogs for replacements. 'Bonica', my bubblegum cutie, was replaced with a new 'Bonica'—an obvious choice. I yanked out the dead 'Knock Out' and put in 'Cuthbert Grant' from Canada's new Parkland series, the government-funded successor to its famous Explorers. Henry Marshall, an amateur gardener, was the genius behind the Parklands, the complex hybrids that carry a trace of Canada's tough, homely, low-growing prairie rose (*Rosa arkansana*) in their genetic mix. The real-life Cuthbert Grant was a leader of Canada's Métis Nation, descendants of indigenous Indians and European settlers (his father was from Scotland).

'Cuthbert' the rose is unusual, to put it mildly. Mine came dormant and on its own roots—a necessity for winter hardiness—via Jung in Wisconsin, a company that doesn't mess with finicky prima donnas. During its first month in residence 'Cuthbert' did nothing above the soil line while its roots settled in. Then it broke dormancy and quickly exploded with large, double, red blooms that turned purple-red as they matured. Even better, its leafy canes stretched out in all directions, a feat Radler's 'Knock Out' had never accomplished. Best of all, 'Cuthbert''s flowers exceed three inches in size, a record for roses on my terrace, and a single bloom looks magnificent in a bud vase.

By the end of May, 'The Fairy' was producing enough new growth from the base for me to let it live on; I filled out its tub with volunteer portulaca. Alas, the trio of 'Nathalie Nypels' gave up trying; they were replaced with three new ones from the Antique Rose Emporium in Texas. All my roses survived the wretched freeze-thaws that I call the non-spring of 2016, which nearly did in my favorite hydrangea.

BUTTERFLIES IN THE GARDEN

Butterfly bushes do attract butterflies. So does the annual heliotrope, the dwarf annual chrysanthemum 'Snowdrop', and in a pinch, coreopsis. The list of butterfly magnets goes on for many pages; here I am mentioning only the plants I've grown.

I was not thinking of butterflies when I searched for a summer-flowering bush of reasonable proportions to replace my late, lamented peach tree. I chose a *Buddleia* (the butterfly bush's botanical name) because it is tough and wind resistant. In my youthful bikini and beachcombing summers on Fire Island I'd noticed its lavender trusses reaching over the tops of walled yards. Towering buddleias grow wild in the Himalayas; garden buddleias are bred for a smaller size and a wider color range. Some gardeners dislike the shrub for its rampant, tenacious growth; I bet they haven't gardened on sandy Fire Island or a high city terrace. In midsummer, the flowers mature sequentially on long panicles, producing sugary nectar with a sweet scent I can't detect but other folks and butterflies can.

'Nanho Purple', the smallest cultivar I could find, was developed from a Chinese subspecies by the Boskoop breeding program in Holland and came to me via Jung's catalog in Wisconsin, a transnational path that is typical in horticulture. The quart pot of roots and dried foliage spread rapidly into a cascade of woody stems bearing long leaves and trusses of purple flowers with bright orange eyes. The following spring I cut the buddleia back to six inches, as recommended, and I've cut it back severely every spring since then. In its second summer, 'Nanho Purple' began to attract orange-and-black Monarchs. I was astonished. The butterfly invasion around here starts in July and lasts for about two weeks. Of course, when I wanted to double-check my timetable this summer, I

Buddleia

didn't see any Monarchs; however, in late August there was an excellent group feast by small orange-and-black butterflies I couldn't identify.

Monarchs are restless creatures. I'd say their disposition is unusually energetic and nervous. They swarm, swoop, hover, dart, alight on their spindly feet, suck briefly through a long proboscis, and flit away. My terrace must be one of thousands of pit stops on their journey, so perhaps they don't have time for a longer visit. I'm thrilled to see the Monarchs get nourishment from my butterfly bush, though I sense they are not comfortable with their competition. To my annoyance, and I believe to the butterflies' annoyance, pushy bumblebees suck at the same buddleia. Bumblebees have a foraging range of one to three miles. I'm not sure where my bumblebees are nesting, but I do know they are greedy guzzlers that buzz from one flower to another to imbibe nectar and accidentally collect the pollen that sticks to their feet. They hassle my salvia, attack my coreopsis, maul the

Campanula

campanula, and wriggle into the penstemon's cupped blooms. A bumblebee will pry into an unopened rose; a bumblebee will return no matter
how many times I shoo it away. The bumblebee's accidental role in the
ecosphere is pollination. Bumblebees are daytime insects, on the job before
I step onto the terrace with my morning coffee. They fly back to their nest,
sometimes a simple hole in the ground, before dusk. I am not being snarky
about a hole in the ground—a pile of debris suits a bumblebee just fine.
Sometimes they do sleepovers on the terrace under a leaf.

   If the bumblebees weren't enough aggravation, my butterfly bush
now attracts honeybees as well. The new invaders horned in when an
outgoing mayor known for his imperial arrogance decided to burnish
his legacy by legalizing honeybee hives on city rooftops. Honeybee
hives are a hobby for some folks and a moneymaking scheme for others. From my extensive personal observation I can state that honeybees

are smaller than bumblebees, aren't fuzzy, and have transparent wings unlike their bumblebee cousins. I did some reading on the division of labor in honeybee hives. When the foragers' stomach sacs are engorged with nectar, they fly back to the hive and regurgitate the load so the stay-at-home worker bees can reduce the water content by flapping their wings. The hive worker bees have a second crucial skill. They make beeswax to build the hexagonal cells of their honeycomb so the thickened nectar can be stored for their food. *Not so fast, honeybees! Your hive owner can't wait to paste labels on his jars of your honey!* And nobody asked me or any other city gardener if we want our lovingly tended flowers to be part of the scheme.

So many innocents are unaware that all bees destroy flowers. Honeybee hive propagandists downplay this inconvenient fact. They would rather scare us by talking about "colony collapse disorder" as if it were one of the major ecological crises of our time. What I know is that wherever a bee sucks, a flower dies—its petals shrivel and turn brown; if the flower has not reached the petal stage, it never will. That is the larger truth about nature. Who speaks for the flowers? If summoned before a magistrate's court would a flower agree that it's perfectly fair for it to die aborning for the greater good of the survival of the species? I don't see the flower conceding. A flower of mine would not concede. Bumblebees and honeybees belong in the country where flowers are destroyed so others may be pollinated and honey may be made. Neither type of bee belongs in a city where every flower is precious and butterflies are always welcome.

Scientists have isolated more than thirty chemical compounds in the buddleia's rich nectar, which attracts hummingbirds and night-flying moths as well. Night-flying moths come in droves to feast on my butterfly bush while I am sleeping—I know this because the morning after a night-flying moth attack I see the remains of their bacchanal. Sometimes I see a laggard night-flying moth in the daytime. It looks

Heliotrope

Lavender

like a homely butterfly and is related to the butterfly, but its colors are dull and its wings hang down in an awkward V-shape when it rests.

When the Monarchs first arrived, my black cat was beside himself at the joy of catching this new prey and bringing it indoors. It was a bitter, mismatched game for the captured Monarch, and a horror for me to witness a dying butterfly flap the denuded scaffolds of its wings on my carpet. Through a PBS television documentary I learned that some Monarchs in the northeastern United States and Canada migrate in stages to a warm winter home in central Mexico, guided by celestial navigation, magnetic fields, and a circadian clock in the butterfly's brain. Their journey is imperiled by losses along the way from exhaustion, difficult weather, limited sources of nectar, and from cats. The Monarch was the first butterfly that was lured to my terrace, but other butterfly species arrived when I extended my planting range to include a dwarf heliotrope. For years I'd wanted to grow purple heliotrope because it was the favorite flower of Babe Paley, the fashionable socialite on all the Best Dressed lists and the wife of a CBS executive known for his television smarts and his philandering. It's odd what we take away from biographies and bring to the garden.

Heliotrope, famed for its vanilla scent, is a tender perennial from South America that is started in a greenhouse for use as an annual here. The Paleys, as you'd expect, had a private greenhouse. I'd never seen a heliotrope until the dwarf cultivar 'Marine' appeared early one May at our local farmers' market. I grabbed it, breaking my no-annuals-before-Mother's-Day rule. While I was in a buying mode, I picked up three plants of the dwarf chrysanthemum 'Snowland' and some apricot sweet alyssum to use as filler.

Right after I tucked the chrysanthemums into their station, under-planted them with the alyssum, and potted out the dwarf heliotrope 'Marine', it started to rain. Cold, heavy rain for days on end. I knew it was a mistake to plant annuals before Mother's Day. When a break in the weather finally came, I ventured onto the terrace. So did a small butterfly. The dainty charmer swooped onto a chrysanthemum for a little suck and then flitted to the heliotrope for a blissful extended feeding. I couldn't believe my good fortune, and neither could the dainty charmer, for I saw it return to the heliotrope two days later.

While the butterfly fed, I had plenty of time to jot down its shape and markings: scalloped triangular wings with a black-striped border along the top and blue dots along the bottom; underside of wings dull and irregularly patterned; prominent antennae and a rather big furry body for such a diminutive creature. A surge of empathy came over me for this solitary, hungry stranger. Several times a day I'd charge onto the terrace to stare in vain at the heliotrope while I waited for the elegant

Monarch butterfly

little butterfly to return. I recognized the signs of a teenage crush. I
needed to know the charmer's name.

After numerous investigations into butterfly books and online
butterfly sites, I am prepared to say that my dainty visitor was a Small
Tortoiseshell, a member of the brushfoot (Nymphalidae) family that
is adored in Europe and Britain. The Small Tortoiseshell is among
the first butterflies to appear in the spring and is so calm and friendly
around humans that one British writer, obviously a dog lover, dubbed
it "the Labrador of the butterfly world." The Small Tortoiseshell is
not an American native. Apparently it came to New York and other
parts of this country with "human assistance," in the diplomatic words
of Wikipedia. Perhaps it arrived in a box of butterflies that some
companies sell for release at wedding celebrations. I hope it establishes
itself here. Somewhere in the vicinity (I have no idea of its range),
this winsome guest may be hosted through its egg, caterpillar, and
chrysalis stages in a patch of nettles, if there are still patches of nettles

in New York City, for nettles are the natural habitat in which the Small Tortoiseshell breeds.

I do not care to grow nettles on my terrace. I continue to grow a heliotrope annually. If I bury my nose right into it, I get an intoxicating whiff of vanilla.

My butterfly saga has a coda. During the summer of 2016, a black butterfly with a blue edge swooped onto the terrace from the rooftop garden above me. It showed no interest in the butterfly bush on several return visits. I thought that was odd.

On August 30, I dashed off a Facebook post: "I was alarmed this morning to see five large caterpillars in my parsley plant. I've always grown parsley, but I've never had caterpillars." The conversation went on for the better part of a week—with an offer of a web cam—while I researched "parsley caterpillars" on Google.

I learned that my smooth-skinned invaders—banded in green, yellow, and black, and chewing furiously—had emerged from eggs deposited by a female Black Swallowtail butterfly. (I hadn't noticed the egg stage, or seen the mating.) A pest to some gardeners, the Black Swallowtail is the official butterfly of the state of New Jersey. If she doesn't find a natural habitat, the female may deposit her eggs in cultivated parsley, fennel, or dill. In nature's plan, the caterpillar is supposed to morph into a chrysalis attached to its host plant; the chrysalis morphs into a butterfly, either quickly or after it overwinters.

On the frantic morning that I counted eleven caterpillars on my denuded plant, I rushed to the grocery store for organic fresh-cut parsley to replenish their food supply. Only three caterpillars were in the pot when I came home. Several were marching on the pavers, evidently seeking a new host plant so they might continue their reproductive process. All my caterpillars vanished in less than a week after I first saw them. End of my story, and the end of theirs, I think.

DAYLILY DREAMS

'd seen tall, orange daylilies growing wild along country roads, but not until I studied the *Hemerocallis* pages in garden catalogs did I learn that so much hybridizing was going on in their world. New short cultivars that are perfect for small gardens! Astonishing differences in shapes, colors, and hues! Ruffled! Double! Reblooming! Diploids and tetraploids (double the number of chromosomes) that can't pollinate each other!

Daylilies are not American natives, though they took root in our soil as if they'd been here forever. *Hemerocallis fulva*, our familiar road-side wildling, was collected in China for food and medicine for thou-sands of years. Traders on the Silk Route carried seeds to the Middle East, and from there the proto-daylily migrated to Europe, from where early colonists took the seeds by ship to America, planting them for a bit of color in their front yards and cemeteries, from which the plants escaped.

French horticulturalists were the first to fool around with the chromosomal makeup of the proto-daylily. Oddly enough, the Chinese never went in for hybridizing—I bet they're sorry now. Dried daylily buds are a must-have ingredient in Chinese cuisine, most famously in hot and sour soup. America's fever for hybridizing daylilies took off about eight decades ago, when amateur gardeners with obsessive habits and a scientific streak began crossing and recrossing the plants in their backyards. Local daylily clubs popped up here and there—in Texas, Arizona, Arkansas, Atlanta, and Chicago—to show and trade the new creations. Local and regional associations are still fairly autonomous,

Tetraploid daylily (*back*)

though they affiliate with the American Hemerocallis Society, the umbrella group formed in 1946.

The AHS has registered more than seventy-five thousand daylily cultivars. I've grown fewer than a dozen: 'Mini Pearl' (luminous soft peach); 'Pardon Me' (cranberry); 'Little Grapette' (burgundy); 'Miss Tinkerbell' (salmon pink with a rosy eye zone); one of the Siloams created by the legendary Pauline Henry of Siloam Springs, Arkansas (my Siloam is yellow with a maroon eye zone); 'Early Cardinal' (red with yellow and green throat); and 'Bahama Butterscotch' (a sturdy tetraploid with ruffled caramel edges). The wind did away with the rest of the markers.

'Mini Pearl' was my first daylily, purchased in the mid-1980s. It is housed in a magnificent brown-glazed urn that a neighbor in the building gave me when he knew he was dying of AIDS. His name was

Rodgers, and he was an editor in book publishing who loved plants and liked to hang out on the building's roof deck for the view and the breeze. Rodgers would call down "Water them deeply!" in his basso profundo whenever he spotted me with my hose. Sometimes I bumped into him on the street when my dog and I were taking our late-night walk; on these occasions Rodgers was in black leather and chains. So many people in this apartment building died of AIDS in the 1980s that Harvey, the day doorman, started keeping a memorial list.

In one respect, daylily hybrids are consistent with those wild orange giants of roadsides and ditches. A flower usually lasts for one day, but not to worry, plenty more blooms are on the way. Everything is "yesterday, today, and tomorrow" with daylilies, ideal for a city terrace where any flower's life is doomed to be brief.

Here is the daylily cycle: clumps of grassy leaves push through the soil in the spring. Leafless stalks, called scapes, push up bearing odd-looking buds that elongate to resemble the buds of a true lily, another genus entirely. When the buds color up—this happens quickly—the trumpet-shaped flowers are ready to open. On my morning patrol, I admire the day's blooms and cut off yesterday's spent ones, dashing inside to scrub the stains off my hands. Purple and red pigments cause the worst stains and the squishiest mess. Handicraft enthusiasts say they use the staining power of daylilies to dye wool and Easter eggs, but that far I am unwilling to go. Nor do I intend to dry my precious daylily buds for a homemade hot and sour soup. Toward the end of July, the march of the daylilies is over. A sad moment. I pull out the dried scapes and monitor the remaining green ones that have formed pods. More about pods later.

Oakes Daylilies in Tennessee, a family business, is where I order my plants because they offer so many choices that don't exceed the eighteen-inch height limit that is best for a pot on a terrace. I can tell they're amused when I phone in my order—"One plant, please"—and explain that I garden in a New York City highrise. Oakes mails me a large, air-dried clump of several divisions, or fans, with huge roots they've dug from their fields. Once they sent me a gift clump of a repeat bloomer. Another time they mailed me two daylilies for the price of one. I don't know why Oakes is so generous—I'm hardly a valuable customer, especially since I propagated a hybrid on my own.

I became an accidental breeder of daylilies, courtesy of the wind, after a curious green pod developed on a scape that had finished blooming. Clearly (well, it's clear to me now), one of my daylilies had pollinated another of my daylilies in the stamens and pistils thing we learn about in school. I rushed to the Web and found I had viable seed in a "one parent unknown" situation. Following the published instructions, I waited until the pod hardened before I cracked it open, teased out the shiny black seeds and put them in a paper envelope that I stored in my fridge's vegetable bin. In April, I took out the seeds, put them in a glass of water for three days to plump them up for easier germination, and then planted them outdoors, where in short order small clumps of daylily leaves arose. One year later I had flowers. Then I had to divide the clumps because I had planted five seeds to a pot.

Even if you know both parents, the results of a cross are uncertain. Forget the phrase, "They're like two peas in a pod." Seeds in a pod are like a mixed litter of puppies—you don't know how the genetic material is combined and what you will get.

The American Hemerocallis Society has stiff requirements for registering an original creation. The line between amateurs and professionals is not firmly drawn, though "one parent unknown" crosses are not in the running. Serious hybridizers hand-brush the pollen from one daylily's stamens onto another daylily's pistil, wrap and tag the receiving partner, and always take notes. A hybridizer might make a

'Miss Tinkerbell'

thousand crosses and recrosses before a new daylily is deemed worthy of registration. It must have a unique quality, a high bud count, good branching, stable color, flower stalks held well above foliage, and other positive merits. When daylily fever hit me, my dream was to propagate something absolutely smashing by dumb luck, and proudly give divisions to my gardening friends. So far what the wind and I have wrought has not been smashing. The truth is, I've never bred a new daylily that compares to the rugged beauties I've purchased from Oakes, but once I came close.

A few years ago 'Bahama Butterscotch', the lone tetraploid on my terrace, bred by Elizabeth Salter in Florida, and the jauntiest, brightest, strongest, longest-blooming daylily I tend, threw me for a loop by producing a seedpod at the end of its flowering season. *What?* Tets are 44-chromosome conversions from 22-chromosome diploids, created by elaborate means involving colchicine, a chemical found naturally in crocuses. Only a tet can pollinate a tet, but some tets can pollinate themselves. Breathless in wonder, I planted five of the tet's seeds in a pot. One year later—I was running out of available pots—I pulled out four of the grassy clumps and saved the strongest one, which happened to be in the middle. The remaining clump sent up one flowering stalk that was a near replica of 'Bahama Butterscotch' with its ruffled dark caramel edges. The following year it sent up three stalks with butterscotch flowers that had disappointingly faint ruffled caramel edges. But I loved it—I was there at the creation. Recently it died.

'Mini Pearl', my first daylily from the 1980s, is doing poorly, so I've got a dilemma. Do I buy a new 'Mini Pearl' with luminescent soft peachy flowers, or do I try a new, bold tetraploid in another color for the brown glazed pot that Rodgers gave me? I need to make a decision soon.

A PEONY BUSH

They are fleeting spring bloomers, and space on my terrace is at such a premium that I had room for only one peony bush three decades ago when I decided to try one, and that peony had to be short. Some beauties I craved, like 'Festiva Maxima', a classic white with inner traces of red, were out of the question—their tall stems would flop in the wind. After much research and mulling over, I planted a three-eyed division of *Paeonia* 'Edulis Superba' that arrived via mail order from Jung in Wisconsin. 'Edulis Superba' has voluptuous double blooms of old-rose pink that hide gold stamens at their center, and it is only two-and-a-half feet tall. Hybridized in France from a Chinese species, this peony, introduced in 1824, proved so tough and dependable that it is still in cultivation today. 'Edulis' is so common that many catalogs don't list it. A peony bush, I've read, can stay productive for one hundred years, maybe longer. As De Beers says about diamonds, a peony is forever.

You don't need a sentimental association with peonies to love them, although many gardeners say they are emotionally attached to the old peonies they saw in their parents' yards. My family in Brooklyn did not have a yard, but I can vividly recall a bouquet of peonies wrapped in cellophane and ribbons that marked a crucial passage during my preteen years. The era of weekly piano lessons and a daily hour of practicing with a metronome for girls who longed to be playing jump rope or riding a bike coincided with the era of the upright spinet for families that could not afford a full-size piano or find the space for one in a small apartment. That was my family. Mr. Gordon, the third and last of my piano teachers to give me a weekly lesson, held an annual concert at Town Hall in Manhattan where his students performed to the best of their abilities, which in my case wasn't much. After we finished our pieces, we were supposed to take a bow while the audience of parents applauded and an attendant brought out a bouquet the student's mother had purchased.

At my one concert with Mr. Gordon, an older girl brought down the house with the Warsaw Concerto. I stumbled through the Moonlight Sonata, striking a complete run of wrong chords near the end. As I lurched from the piano to take the mandatory bow, Mr. Gordon's assistant rushed up with a huge bunch of long-stemmed peonies—the most glorious bouquet of the afternoon. I remember the freckled deep pinks (*Paeonia* 'Freckles'?) and the sumptuous whites with a trace of red that had to be 'Festiva Maxima'. Mr. Gordon motioned me off the stage, but I was transfixed by the peonies' beauty and stunned by my mother's extravagant gesture. After my sorry performance I was allowed to stop taking lessons, and my mother, who had dearly wished to play the piano all her life, began the metronome and scales routine with Mr. Gordon, and soon she was stumbling through her own rendition of the Moonlight Sonata. We had each achieved what we truly wanted, and peonies remain my favorite flower.

The instructions for planting a peony division are very precise. Fall is the proper time to put a peony into its permanent home; peony authorities are unanimous in their opinion that a peony does not like being uprooted and moved. The long-living plant needs full sun, winter chill, and good air circulation, a cinch on my terrace. The soil should be enriched with peat moss and the eyes must be planted no more than two inches deep. (I was so anxious about hitting the two-inch mark that I used a ruler.) After the first year, a liberal dressing of dried cow manure (yum, all the basic nutrients plus humus to help the roots absorb them) should be applied early each spring. The books said to do it, so I did it. Dried cow manure is increasingly rare in city nurseries; city nurseries have become exceedingly rare, for that matter. The one spring that I didn't spread a coat of manure around 'Edulis' and doused it with Miracle-Gro, which works fine for me on other plants, I got lots of foliage and few flowers. Too much nitrogen in the formula for a peony? Perhaps.

Until recently, I believed that peonies proved the value of ants. I'd been taken in by a popular myth that has finally been debunked. A full, tight peony bud that is showing color, already beautiful in its roundness, will open and bloom whether an ant licks off its sticky resinous surface or not. Ants line up every spring for their chance to lick 'Edulis', and I'd always cheered them on. I was shocked to learn that the peony-ant relationship is not symbiotic. Aside from aerating the soil in their diligent effort to make nests—I'm not scoffing at soil aeration—ants are a nasty presence. I bait them with traps, crush them under my foot, slam them by hand, and spray them with Raid, though never with total success.

Every spring my peony bush provides me with perfect blooms, never fewer than six, to cut and bring into the house. Bringing them indoors is a sensible move because of the wind factor. A peony in bloom on my terrace has a shorter lifespan than it does in a vase in my living room. In fact, the peak condition of a peony bloom on my terrace is approximately one day. I grab them fast, before they are fully open.

Cut peonies are four dollars or more for a single stem in the city, so I have gotten my money's worth from 'Edulis Superba'. On the negative side, a powdery white mildew began to afflict the peony's leaves and stems in the plant's third decade. I try to keep the mildew under control with a fungicide, but to read some online sites is to get alarmed: airborne spores of powdery white mildew feed on the plant's tissue; the fungus will always recur if the spores get into the soil; marijuana, tomato, and rose growers struggle mightily against powdery white mildew (marijuana growers are particularly vocal online); the fungus began to attack peonies fairly recently; spores for the peony fungus are "host specific," meaning they don't attack roses, tomatoes, or marijuana leaves, and vice versa, but spores on a peony bush are bound to attack another peony. *What beautiful peony somewhere in Greenwich Village got infected before mine did?* I'm beginning to think I should start over with a new pot, fresh soil, and a new 'Edulis', or go whole hog and try another cultivar altogether.

Update: The terrible winter and nonexistent spring of 2014–2015 wreaked havoc on 'Edulis', which did not bloom. When autumn came, I prepared a new pot with fresh soil and planted the roots of another short oldie, the cherry-red double 'Karl Rosenfield' introduced in 1908 by J. P. Rosenfield, a Swedish immigrant who settled in Nebraska where he developed and purveyed his Chinese hybrids. J. P. named 'Karl Rosenfield' for his son, so maybe he thought this peony would be his legacy. If so, he was right. It is the only Rosenfield peony to remain in cultivation today, because of its popularity in the cut-flower business. I swear I never saw 'Karl Rosenfield' in the catalogs for home growers that I used to read like religious tracts. The root mass I purchased on eBay, where many plant sellers have set up shop, arrived in a cereal box, a nice homey touch.

Unbothered by the next year's delayed, frigid spring in 2016, the wine-colored stems of 'Karl Rosenfield' emerged with astonishing vigor. (Emerging peony stems are usually wine-colored before they green up.) The solitary cherry-red double bloom that young 'Karl' deigned to bring forth was packed so intensely with petals that I got out my camera for a photo session. Over in its pot thirty feet away, the less vigorous 'Edulis Superba' also sent up one solitary bloom. I have not had the heart to trash 'Edulis', not yet. This is irrational of me, or perhaps just unduly sentimental. Young 'Karl' is a sitting duck for the powdery white mildew spores that afflicted 'Edulis'. Agh.

HYDRANGEAS

Hydrangeas are famously romantic: swooned over by the French and Martha Stewart, starring as table decorations for wedding dinners, potted and wrapped in gilt paper for Mother's Day, paraded in tall vases or tucked into low bowls at fine restaurants, silkscreened for lush wallpaper patterns. My bathroom is papered in a hydrangea pattern, and my kitchen window frames the living, incomparable 'Nikko Blue', a tough, big-leafed mophead I've fussed over for decades because—oh gee, because a hydrangea in bloom is so dreamy.

H. macrophylla is native to Japan, where it thrives in coastal regions buffeted by wind and salt spray, so it stood to reason that a *macrophylla* hydrangea might tolerate a windy terrace near a river. Not all *macrophylla* hybrids can tolerate wind. Before 'Nikko' arrived from Wayside Gardens, I had tried 'Otaksa', which didn't make it. 'Nikko Blue' began its journey with me in a low wood box on the south side of the terrace, where it managed to grow and bloom in full sun. I shouldn't have imposed such a wretched beginning on 'Nikko'—I knew perfectly well from my reading that hydrangeas require some shade and do best in morning sun and afternoon shade, but a low wood box on the sunny south side was the only station available at the time. A few summers into our cooperative venture, I could no longer ignore my hydrangea's need for shade and its desperate hunt for more room. The unfortunate shrub wilted every afternoon unless it was watered twice daily, and, as if I needed another warning, its cramped roots were poking through the slats of its wood box.

'Nikko Blue'

These disturbing events coincided with the decline, from a cottony fungus, of my spring flowering crabapple that occupied a semi-shaded corner on the north side of the terrace. The crabapple had given me many good years, and the birds of fall had enjoyed feasting on its berry-size red fruits, but its number was up. I asked the building's porters to saw it down and remove its box. When 'Nikko' started to go dormant, shedding its leaves for its winter sleep, I executed a plan to house it in the tree's vacated space, in a new commodious polyurethane urn. Not that the move from south side to north side went off without a hitch. Delivered at the end of the workday from a store in the city's wholesale flower district, the polyurethane urn could not fit through the terrace door however it was angled. The deliveryman was as upset as I was. I proposed that we lower the urn from the roof, a procedure I vividly recalled from the time when the heavy tubs for the birches were

H. quercifolia 'Snow Queen'

brought in. I did the lowering, and the deliveryman, waiting below, did the catching. Sighing in relief, he offered to extend his duties, a proposal I gratefully accepted. After filling the urn with fresh potting soil, he freed 'Nikko' from its decrepit box—the wood slats offered no resistance—and plunked the hydrangea's root mass into its new home. Local deliverers of garden products, I've found, often enjoy the chance to do some gardening. Over the man's chivalrous objections, I insisted on finishing the job myself. I firmed the plant in, added more soil, and flooded the urn with plenty of water. 'Nikko' leafed out the following spring—the transplant was a success.

Its new home did not fit the hydrangea's optimum requirements for morning sun and afternoon shade, but it provided morning shade and roomy quarters. When 'Nikko' leafs out in late March or April, I scratch a few spoonfuls of aluminum sulfate into the soil. Flower buds consisting of tiny lime-green florets appear at the tops of its leafy branches in May; the tightly packed florets begin to show color when the flower heads quadruple in size. Waiting for 'Nikko' to color up makes me anxious. In addition to the aluminum sulfate, I water the hydrangea from time to time with an acidifying plant food so its roots can absorb the aluminum, a requisite for a blue hydrangea if it is going to produce blue flowers. I don't want them turning pink, the fate of blue hydrangeas that are aluminum-deprived. Under my ministrations, the mopheads are a mix of sky blue and dusky purple.

My pruning timetable goes like this: late in the fall when the plant has lost most of its leaves, I cut back some of the towering stalks by a third of their height—going against the advice of the experts who warn not to cut back a hydrangea in the fall because it produces flowers in the spring only on old growth. Please, I know what works best for my hydrangea; I do not want a giant; I need a manageable plant. Early in the spring, I thin out the skinny, weak stalks, remove the dead ones, and cut off the shriveled winterkill to a strong, scaly, outward-facing bud. Then the ordained process of leafing and flowering begins anew. 'Nikko' expanded from a wilting two-footer to four feet high and wide in its northwest corner facing the river. Its large, serrated leaves are strong and shiny; its five-inch mopheads of tightly packed florets range from periwinkle blue to dusky violet. 'Nikko' is awesome. It glories in rainstorms. Sometimes I go up to the roof just to peer down on my pride and joy from another perspective, to marvel at the way this hydrangea adjusts into a symmetrical mound as it produces new blooms through August, September, even into October, though the last little flower heads do not get to mature when the temperature hits freezing.

Macrophylla hydrangeas are pleasing to the eye when they are grown in an urn, and I say this not only because that's the way I must grow one. The urn's height allows the outer flowering stems to dip down gracefully without touching the ground. Of course if you have a huge estate, your fulltime landscapers may grow quantities of hydrangeas that appear to meld into one another in a tapestry pattern—I've seen these incredible displays in the vast gardens of French chateaux—but an intimate relationship with one hydrangea is a grand adventure.

'Nikko Blue' is so exquisite, so perfectly mounded, that I hesitate to cut off a few stems for an indoor display; however, on summer mornings when I do want some cut flowers, I strip off the leaves and refrigerate the stems in water to ease their transition. It is crucial not to cut a hydrangea stem until the flower head is fully colored so it won't wilt. If you think about it, have you ever seen immature, partially colored hydrangeas for sale at a florist? Okay, sometimes. Florists shouldn't do this. Roses and peonies may be cut before they mature, but hydrangea blooms should be mature before they are cut. In autumn I put a bunch of dried mopheads in a vase for memories, where they stay until 'Nikko' starts unfurling its leaves again in the spring. It is truly a shrub for all seasons.

Buoyed by my success with 'Nikko', I extended my hydrangea horizons to *H. quercifolia* 'Snow Queen', which sends up large, pointy white flowers in the spring that turn rosy in the summer if the bees don't get to them first. *Quercifolia* hydrangeas are American natives with coarse, oak-leaf-shaped leaves that look like they can survive anything. This is almost true. Planted in a large wood barrel against the brick wall on the west side of my terrace where the elements are fierce, the 'Snow Queen' has outgrown its station, and its leaves occasionally tear in the wind. But it won my heart by adjusting to its cramped life; its oldest woody stems periodically die to make way for new growth, and in the spring I dig out the blocky dead wood. During the summer, a cut stem of 'Snow Queen' at its rosy stage lasts for a long time in a vase. I am painfully aware that the pointy white flowers on 'Snow Queen' are smaller than they used to be. This super-hardy hydrangea is beginning to resemble a bonsai version of its former self. I wish I had a better location for the 'Snow Queen' to strut its stuff. A sad end game may be in store for this strong hydrangea, but end games are to be expected on a city terrace.

Update: The super-hardy 'Snow Queen' survived the horrific winter and frigid spring of 2014–2015 to produce two small flower heads. My champion 'Nikko Blue' almost succumbed. Its dieback was awful. I do not wish to tally the number of hours over several weeks that I spent cutting down withered stems and sawing out blocks of dead wood from my pride and joy. The professional garden staff for the terrace across the way gave me looks I interpreted as amused, incredulous, and astonished, but the hard labor was therapeutic for me as well as for 'Nikko'. I could not give up on the hydrangea I'd bonded with so intimately. When 'Nikko' signaled that its roots were still viable—a few tentative green shoots struggled to push up from the soil—I was certain the bush was going to live if I kept my part of the bargain. By August, when 'Nikko' is normally in full bloom, its new shoots were two feet high. I did not expect they would produce any mopheads—'Nikko' flowers on the previous year's wood, I reminded myself—but I was confident the bush would look like itself again the following year.

A surprise lightened my misery while I ministered daily to the recovering 'Nikko'. A neighbor I didn't know with a patio apartment on the second floor got tired of coming home from business trips to dead plants and asked Val, the doorman, to remove his containers. Val asked me if I wanted them. Did I ever! He trundled up four chic, black rectangular troughs and one tall square pot, all minus the neighbor's dead plants but filled with good soil, and spaced them around the sad-looking north side of the terrace where 'Nikko' usually reigned supreme. I hurried to the farmers' market in Union Square wondering what I could find so late in the season, and grabbed four untagged small pink hydrangeas in bloom. On impulse I added three pots of lavender; I discuss them in "Experimental Stations."

With the confidence of Sherlock Holmes, I deduced that the untagged pink hydrangeas were leftovers that had been forced in a greenhouse for the Mother's Day market, though their pots were not wrapped in gilt paper. Knocked out and planted, they settled in and remained modest in size, continuing to flower for the rest of the season. One turned out to be a pink lacecap. I'd yearned for a lacecap after admiring a blue one for several years in the front yard of a townhouse on my street. Lacecaps have flat centers surrounded by a ring of petals and are supposed to be smaller and hardier than conventional mopheads. My mysterioso hydrangeas might all be eight-footers: I don't expect them to flourish in their low troughs for many years, but they're nice to have around now.

During the dismal spring of 2016, when bitter freezes and north winds hit the city in April and May, the super-hardy 'Snow Queen' in its west side station leafed out without blinking. The three small pink mopheads on the north side leafed out too. The pink lacecap's shriveled stems made me think it had died; I had judged it too quickly. Slowly the lacecap sent up new life from the soil line. It will not flower this year, and I'm not sure what its ultimate fate will be.

To my horror, 'Nikko Blue' got seriously flummoxed by this second disastrous non-spring in a row. Triggered by longer days and warmer weather, my champion had leafed out in triumph. When the freezing winds returned with a vengeance, nine-tenths of its new growth died. A lesson to learn from this tragedy is that plants make mistakes just as humans do, since they can't peer into the future. Another lesson is that stress from two consecutive years of misfortune can reduce a plant's and a human's ability to cope.

And how did the rest of my plants fare on the north side? The honeysuckle 'Major Wheeler' that twines on the parapet railing in close proximity to 'Nikko' survived its leaf damage and sent up two new stems from the soil line. Every flowering stem blew off the *Dicentra* (Bleeding Heart) that occupies a low pot between 'Nikko' and the 'Major'. This beloved longtime occupant of my terrace is always the first to bloom in the spring, and often suffers for it. Happily for me, it produced a second, though smaller, flush. A daylily I'd propagated died.

I still have too much emotion invested in 'Nikko Blue' to part from its company. While I try yet again to nurse the mophead back to its former glory, I am hedging my bets on the pink lacecap's bid for survival by putting a blue lacecap starter plant in the tub where the daylily didn't make it. The newbie is called 'Teller Blue' in this country; in Europe it's 'Blaumeise', named after an adored blue and yellow bird. The Teller series of hardy hydrangeas was developed in Switzerland with government funding. I like knowing stories like that.

MY THIRTY-YEAR GERANIUMS

Greenwich Village had its own garden center on Hudson Street in the 1970s, a laidback place where you could browse along gravel paths and find unexpected treasures. One summer's day I picked up some miniature geraniums. All right, their botanical name is *Pelargonium*, but we all call them geraniums. I'd never seen a miniature geranium before. Most people haven't. Everybody knows the big geraniums because they are everywhere. These were six inches tall and had small zonal geranium leaves and small, lovely geranium flowers of the single kind. The garden center—how I miss it—had two named varieties for sale, each in bicolored hues of salmon and blush. One was more salmon and the other had more blush. Their unimaginative names were 'Pixie' and 'Fairy'. So I bought two pots of each and planted them in a tongue-and-groove redwood box. In the cheerful habit of geraniums, they prospered and multiplied, blooming their fool heads off, undaunted by the wind.

At the end of the season I couldn't bear to part with these little gems. I dug them up, divided and trimmed their tangled roots into manageable clumps, sheared off some fleshy stems that had grown thick and ungainly, and plunked the mini geraniums into small plastic pots with fresh soil, watering them thoroughly to avert trauma. I hoped the minis might winter-over indoors on a sunny windowsill, and perhaps continue to flower. It was touch-and-go for a while. The plants lost some leaves and required frequent misting to cope with the hot radiator beneath their shelf, but they adapted and did continue to flower, a bit wanly.

Bicolored geranium

After Mother's Day, my fail-safe date usually beyond danger from a sudden frost, I set the mini geraniums out again, meticulously abiding by an expert's hardening-off process. On the first day the pots were allowed one hour outdoors in a shady spot. On the second day they were permitted two hours, etc. At the end of the week they had their first overnight and were ready for planting. I enriched the soil in the redwood box, dug the appropriate holes, knocked the geraniums out of their pots, spread their roots, and returned them to their summer home.

I've been hewing to this "geraniums in, geraniums out" routine for thirty years, although far less meticulously than I used to. One November I waited too long to execute the intake maneuver and

'Telstar'

most of the plants froze. One May I said to hell with hardening-off and set out the plants without any prep time. They suffered, but they recovered. I'd root fresh cuttings by dipping the little stems in Rootone, a hormone powder, before I stuck them in little pots of fresh soil and bagged them in plastic to keep up the humidity. Then I discovered that the little cuttings could root in water without the Rootone and then be transferred to little pots. There are years when I don't propagate by stem cuttings at all, and then I have a thick stem problem and taller mini geraniums to set out. Along the way my two varieties of bicolored salmon and blush became indistinguishable and I don't know which one I lost, nor does it matter.

What does matter is that mini and dwarf geraniums, a nitpicker's distinction, aren't available at garden centers in America today, while humongous geraniums are all over the place. Big geraniums are an easy answer for summer color, but the small ones are so special, so perfect for a city terrace, and so hard to find. Evidently their niche is too small for big business. Very late one evening when I was surfing the Web, I found an online source—a one-woman operation called Hobbs Farm run by Lorraine Smith with the help of her husband, in rural Maine. I snapped up her four remaining 'Telstars' and was so excited that I nearly cried.

The 'Telstars' did nothing but generate foliage during their first summer on the terrace. I took them in for their winter sojourn on the same sunny window ledge where the 'Pixies' (or the 'Fairies') overwinter, and set them out in their own containers the following spring. They surprised me by blooming nonstop. Their color also surprised me. They were deep rose according to Lorraine Smith's description; my 'Telstars' are a vivid cardinal-red. Maybe they're not 'Telstars'. Maybe it's my potting soil versus Lorraine Smith's potting soil. I am not complaining. I now grow two very different looking mini geraniums and in some years have enough to share.

Memo to self: Best month to take mini geranium cuttings is August.

MY IRIS EXPERIENCE

I used to avoid spring-blooming perennials, except for my adored peony bush, because I wanted color all over the place from spring to fall, but now I am willing to go for fleeting joy in a few eighteen-inch pots that I keep around for what strikes my fancy. If I hadn't relaxed my rule about ephemeral bloomers, I'd have missed the chance to witness the growth habits of many celebrated beauties.

Cut irises from a florist give three days of pleasure, max. Grow-your-own irises offer weeks of nail-biting suspense followed by a few days of thrilling rewards followed by interesting-enough foliage for the rest of the year, thanks to breeders who recognize the height and width restrictions of today's smaller gardens.

Overwhelmed by the numerous offerings from Schreiner's, the iris king, I chose a two-footer named 'Batik' from Jung that I figured might do okay in a pot. Jung in Wisconsin specializes in plants that are easy growers; the catalog called 'Batik' a "novelty iris," which I found amusing since any iris I'd grow would be novel to me. I planted the rhizome with clipped leaves in the fall, the proper season for 'Batik' to settle in and make some growth. New blades of iris leaves promptly emerged and held their own through the winter. In May, six huge purple flowers streaked with white opened in sequence on a single stalk.

For a first-time iris grower, 'Batik' was a bonanza, an education, and I must say, a giggle. Its splashes of white on purple reminded me of a tie-dye shirt I'd once bought in India. In my ignorance I mistook the fuzzy yellowish strips on its lower petals for dormant caterpillars until I tried to scrape one off. Enlightenment came with a couple of online clicks. Ah, so—'Batik' was a bearded iris, a famous classification in the iris family, much hybridized, that I'd never seen under the bamboo awnings at the local delis where I often buy seasonal flowers.

In its second year 'Batik' produced seven stalks of huge, bearded hippie tie-dye flowers, as it continues to do every spring in its shameless flamboyance. On the negative side, its top-heavy stalks can flop in a rainstorm. On the plus side, if I put my nose right into a bloom, I am transported by the scent of sugar candy.

One overcast day I went with friends to the Presby Memorial Iris Gardens in New Jersey, the first time I'd seen masses of irises in a field. Presby's curator had stationed herself in an open shed to greet visitors who'd traveled hundreds of miles with wrapped blooming stalks from old yards, hoping an expert could identify their heirloom treasures. Cheekily, I joined the line to inquire about my iris—in my excitement I blanked on its name.

"Uh, I call it the hippie tie-dye iris."

"'Batik'?" she replied without missing a beat. I thanked her and fled.

'Batik' and its ilk are known as broken-color irises. The result of genetic instability, their splishes and splashes are irregular, even on one stalk, a phenomenon that made me feel I had done something wrong until I did further reading. Some iris growers call broken-color hybrids weirdoes and oddballs, and they adore them. Allan Ensminger, a founder of the Lincoln, Nebraska, Iris Society, introduced 'Batik' in 1986. In his day job, he managed a hydraulics division for Goodyear Tire and Rubber. In his life as an iris hybridizer, his buddies affectionately called him "The Wizard of Odds."

My success with 'Batik' astounded me, but it made me yearn for a refined and demure purple iris without a beard. I freed up a pot and planted the two-foot Siberian 'Ruffled Velvet', introduced in 1980 by Dr. Currier McEwen of Harpswell, Maine. Dr. McEwen was a rheumatologist and a former dean of New York University's School of Medicine who began hybridizing when he was sixty. His 'Ruffled Velvet', the winner of many distinguished awards and medals, looks delicate but is strong. 'Ruffled Velvet' doesn't have any frou-frous, just a finely etched gold pattern at the center of its downward petals, or "falls." (In iris nomenclature, a language of its own, upward petals are "standards" and downward petals are "falls.")

After gleaning what I could about the creators of my two irises (obsessive habits; understanding spouses; productive into their nineties), I felt I was missing something. You make your crosses, you wrap and tag your iris receivers, and you take careful notes, but how do you launch your iris into the world? I got the lowdown from a commercial distributor after I promised not to reveal my source.

Iris hybridizing is a seductive hobby, but you must engage in serious politicking to push your iris along. You start by joining the American Iris Society; then you organize a branch in your hometown and get active in the regional groups. You build a sufficient stock of your hybrid. You make friends with iris lovers on various levels of the AIS hierarchy who judge and award medals to new creations. You register your iris with the AIS and give it a provisional name—you can't name your nearly black hybrid 'Best Black Ever' or something else that is blatantly pushy and open to question. You fill in a sheet detailing your hybrid's parentage: its pod parent and pollen parent as far back as they can be traced. If you get a green light from the AIS, your friends in iris circles who publish small sales catalogs will list your creation with a description and price. Commercial sellers with thick, glossy catalogs and giant direct mailings pore over the small catalogs; if a new iris appeals to them, they buy three specimens and observe how the iris performs in their own fields for several years. If all goes brilliantly, a

'Batik'

big commercial catalog lists your iris with a beautiful photo, and a new star is born.

Hybridizers make no money from their iris's stardom beyond its purchase price in the small catalog where it caught the eye of a commercial giant. What the hybridizers basically get is the joy of seeing their iris pictured among the big shots and the satisfaction of basking in its reflected glory. There are a few additional perks and opportunities. New-to-the-fold hybridizers are invited to speak at regional meetings; they may be asked to write articles for iris publications. Of course they create more iris hybrids, and sometimes lightning strikes again, as it did many times for Dr. McEwen.

The etched pattern on McEwen's 'Ruffled Velvet' looks like a heraldic design. Some historians of heraldry believe that the gold fleur-de-lis, associated with the French monarchy, is a stylized iris. Others maintain that the fleur-de-lis is a stylized lily. Whatever. For a treat, I bought my iris collection—that is, my pots of 'Batik' and 'Ruffled Velvet'—a low-nitrogen fertilizer that irises are said to thrive on. I keep forgetting to use it. Maybe I'll remember next spring.

RIOTOUS ANNUALS

The older I get, the more I appreciate grab-and-plant annuals. Every spring I deploy a select few that are short in height and long on flower power in various containers for nonstop color until they are done in by a hard frost. I buy the starter packs at the Saturday morning Abingdon Square farmers' market two streets from my aerie. It's wise to shop early, while the trucks are unloading. Concklin's Orchards of Rockland County is our neighborhood's plant vendor and purveyor of the world's best cider doughnuts. I don't know why Concklin's abandons us after the Memorial Day weekend for another location in the city. We need them here. Neighborhood farmers' markets are so important to city dwellers. Of course I could schlep my cart to the giant market on Union Square, and sometimes I do, but Union Square, where restaurateurs buy their fresh produce, is not a neighborly chitchat experience.

What we in a temperate climate call annuals are usually perennials in tropical and subtropical climates that were "discovered," so to speak, in the eighteenth and nineteenth centuries by European plant hunters, who transported them by ship to botanical gardens in the Western world where they've been hybridized almost beyond recognition.

I am not wedded to a fixed place for my annuals; they go where I feel they are needed. I pot them out on a cloudy day or late in the afternoon, watering them deeply to reduce the shock of being wrenched from their packs only to suffer another shock when I briskly untangle and spread their roots. Sometimes they look like they've been in their pots for only a few hours and sometimes they're already pot-bound.

Gazania

I do not follow the printed advice on the markers for spacing the annuals; I cram them close together for an instant effect. In addition to my small pot deployment I use annuals in one deep, capacious tub that could hold a perennial (shocking!) because the riotous display outside a window is a joy to behold.

"Thriller, filler, spiller" compositions have lots of adherents. The idea is to plant annuals with three different growing habits in one container; I've seen some excellent results from this method on my walks in the city. A tall plant in the middle is the thriller, or focal point; smaller plants, the fillers, circle the thriller; and trailing plants that hang over the edge are the spillers. I tried "thriller, filler, spiller" once, choosing the vigorous sweet potato vine as my spiller, and it took over the show. I never tried a threesome again, not because of the rambunctious potato vine—I just prefer to grow one kind of annual in one pot.

After decades of ignoring marigolds from unwarranted snobbishness—too common, too zingy, in no way romantic—I am thrilled to grow a carpet of dwarfs, bushy and rarely more than one foot high, that the W. Atlee Burpee seed company introduced as "French" in the 1920s. The tightly packed petals of the two-inch blooms obscure their serrated foliage in bold orange and russet puffs, yellow and russet puffs, and single-color puffs of orange or yellow. French botanists pioneered in hybridizing dwarf marigolds, and French master gardeners were the first to use them as bedding plants in formal parterres, but nothing is intrinsically "French" about these shorties. "African," a label applied to tall, upright marigolds, the originals of the species, is another misnomer. If you wish, you may call all marigolds *Tagetes*, the scientific moniker bestowed on them by Linnaeus, but why would you?

Native to the warmer parts of the Americas, marigolds have been adopted in far-flung places where often they play a spiritual role. They are festooned on graves for Day of the Dead ceremonies in Mexico, where they may have originated. In India, a country that took to marigolds with unbridled passion, the petals are scattered on Hindu shrines during religious festivals, and the flowers are strung into garlands that are draped over dignitaries' shoulders. Indira Gandhi, I remember from seeing on television, would get annoyed with the overload and wave off the garland drapers when her tolerance reached its limit. And then there's *The Best Exotic Marigold Hotel*, the British movie about retirees finding late love that was filmed in Jaipur, a marigold-happy city. In this country, David Burpee, the son of W. Atlee, was such a marigold zealot during the 1960s that he lobbied in Washington to have them declared our national flower, an honor that went to the rose.

I don't bother with marigold seeds, though some people I know harvest them for sowing the following spring—the shiny black-and-white needles look totally different from other seeds I'm acquainted with. Come spring, I buy the rugged cuties in packs when they are bursting with buds and all they need to carry on is sun, warmth, and water, plus deadheading to rid them of blooms that are past their prime, a crucial task that encourages new buds and flowers. Some gardeners consider the pungent smell of marigolds a deal-breaker; I rather like it, and I thoroughly enjoy riffling through the foliage with my fingers. Withered marigolds are great fun to deadhead, which I wouldn't say for most other flowers. Snap off a spent marigold and hear a pop. A highly audible pop. *Pop, pop*, off with their heads! A tub brimming with marigolds that are vigilantly deadheaded can survive a couple of fall frosts.

On impulse one spring I grabbed three gazania starters to fill a planter I'd earmarked for a perennial. To be honest, I'd confused gazania with gaillardia, a perennial on American prairies that I came to know later and disliked. Anyway, the gazanias bloomed beyond my expectations, though the elegant three-inch flowers were a gleaming orange and my terrace had enough orange with the marigolds I was tending. A few weeks later I returned to the market and spied some vanilla gazanias for sale. What was this? I'd assumed gazanias were always yellow or orange, but the wonders of selective breeding have

Marigolds (*front*)

extended their palette to purple, pink, and vanilla, even red, plus contrasting stripes.

Mr. Concklin, our neighborhood vendor, was selling six to a pack; I muttered that I had room only for three. I wasn't haggling, I was just thinking aloud. It was late in the day, and he probably wanted to reload his truck and go home. He presented me with the whole pack as a gift. I became a gazania convert on the spot.

Gazanias are native to South Africa's coastal sand dunes and alpine meadows, so they can tolerate droughts and wind, but they won't tolerate a New York winter and must be treated as disposable annuals. Gazanias are quirky. Let me edit that sentence to say that *my* gazanias appear quirky. Their petals typically close at night and open at daybreak. My gazanias close like clockwork at night, but during the spring they do not open until nine or ten in the morning. I brooded about their lazy habits until I determined that I'd put them in less than optimal stations.

My gazanias grow in low containers that nestle on the western parapet beneath a huge tub for the 'Bonica' rose. This location is totally sunny for the rose (and for my human height), but it is not totally sunny for the gazanias. Every spring, when the sun makes a low arc as it crosses the sky, the gazanias are stuck in shade for half of the morning—it takes hours for the sun's direct rays to reach them and warm their closed petals into greeting the day. During the summer, when the sun's path in the sky is higher, the gazanias open much earlier. I suppose I could relocate the gazania stations to my southern exposure that always receives morning sun, but the south side is already overcrowded with roses, a butterfly bush, a peony, daylilies, clematis, iris, and some herbs.

A withered gazania may be cut or snapped off. The way it is deadheaded makes no difference to the gazania, but I must say that when I snap one, my fingers get sticky from the ooze of its milky sap, which is really annoying. Furthermore, the decibel level of the snap simply does not compare to a marigold's great, big, satisfying *pop*. What I'm saying is that deadheading gazanias is a chore, not a pleasure, but a tub of blooming gazanias is a great pleasure indeed.

"*What's this?*" I asked at the Union Square market well into the summer when overstocked plants appear at alluring prices. I was holding a stiff paper pot of low, trailing foliage with curious deep purple flowers. Each flower had a semicircle of petals gracing its tiny center, as if a full circle had been sliced in half.

"Fan," a worker replied, as if this name was something I should know.

"Fan? Just plain fan?"

He nodded.

"Does it have a scientific name?"

He checked with his boss and reported back. "*Scaevola.*"

"Oh, of course," I said, telling a fib.

I took the unusual plant home and repotted it in a larger container that I jammed next to an iris that was done flowering for the year. It settled in and spread quickly. New fan-shaped flowers grew from the tops and sides of the older ones. Each fan, composed of five petals, was approximately one inch but a multitude of fans made up for their diminutive size. I was surprised and delighted. The newcomer did not require deadheading and bid its adieu after the first serious frost.

The fan flower (I don't think I'll be calling it *Scaevola*) is a perennial in subtropical Western Australia that has been hybridized for export in recent years. It must be treated as an annual in the American north and is difficult to propagate by seed. I've read online that white fan flowers and mauve fan flowers are available, but purple fan flowers remain the most popular kind. Breeders of fan flowers worry about its limited color spectrum, since novelty is the name of the game in a competitive international market, but I love purple so I'm not worried. I just hope I'll find a pot of this sensation every spring.

While on the subject of purple, I should mention heliotrope, a perennial in Peru where it was "discovered" but is grown as an annual in most of this country. Dwarf heliotrope hybrids are perfect for a sunny highrise terrace in New York like mine. I talk at length about dwarf heliotrope in my chapter on butterflies in the garden because heliotrope is a butterfly magnet. The trick is to find a starter plant that has been grown in a hothouse. 'Marine', with dark purple flowers and a delicious scent of vanilla, is the most popular cultivar among the dwarfs. 'Iowa' is taller and is said to be lavender in cool weather and purple in hot weather and has a winey scent. This spring I'm giving 'Iowa' a try. All heliotropes come with a caveat—they are poisonous if ingested, so do not ingest!

Many summers ago I bought a packet of portulaca 'Grandiflora', a low-growing annual six inches tall and a foot wide that is a ubiquitous fixture in window box gardens. I mixed the tiny black seeds with dry sand as directed, dribbled the contents on bare spots in a few containers, and pressed the mixture in gently. Ever since, there's never been a summer on my terrace without some volunteer portulaca.

A volunteer is a seedling you did not plant but wish to keep; a weed is a seedling you did not plant and do not wish to keep. Portulaca is a very successful volunteer, broadcasting its plentiful seed in autumn, usually via the wind, to set the stage for new seedlings to arise elsewhere the following summer. Portulaca's dispersal powers are legend, its emerging succulent leaves are easy to recognize, and its one-inch cup-shaped flowers, single or double, are profuse and pretty. The plants need no deadheading or cutting back unless the stems become long and scraggly.

Flowering portulaca, related to the purslane family, is native to Brazil and Argentina and performs best in a dry, sunny climate. Two hundred years ago, John Gillies, an amateur Scottish botanist, collected its seeds in the sandy soil of the Andes foothills and sent them by ship, along with various cacti, to W. J. Hooker, Glasgow's eminent plant classifier, kicking off its subsequent travels around the globe.

Today's portulaca hybrids have been improved to stay open on cloudy days, and they come in shades of rose, scarlet, salmon, pink, orange, yellow, and white; sometimes they have patterned faces. Mine seed themselves with abandon in the narrow spaces between the pavers on my terrace and sometimes in the daylily pots. Early in the summer, the yellows and whites are the first to appear—I pull and discard them and wait for the shades of rose, pink, and red that I know will follow. What I don't know, frankly, is whether each summer's fresh crop of volunteers are from my portulacas or from seeds that have wafted up from other people's gardens. What I do know is that I can lift the seedlings and tuck them into a sunny spot where fillers are needed, and they will flourish. Most recently I employed them to fill out the tub for my 'Fairy' rose that had barely survived a cruel winter.

Nobody's written a great ode to portulaca; its flowers are pert, dainty, and most welcomed, but they do not rise to the level of poetry. So I composed a ditty: "Portulaca! Portulaca! I'm so pleased that I've got ya!"

I did not include miniature geraniums (*Pelargonium*) in this romp through my favorite annuals because mini geraniums have been so important to my gardening life for thirty years that they have their own chapter.

BOSTON IVY

Boston ivy was the first vine I ever planted, in two narrow, custom-made wood boxes, very deep, that fitted into a small recess on the northwest side of the terrace. The ivy meandered along the harsh redbrick walls, turned a corner to spread on the long western expanse, and was aiming to turn yet another corner and into the climbing rose on the south side—at that time the vigorous pale pink 'New Dawn'. Armed with my Felco pruner and an eight-foot pruning pole with a pulley and cords, I made sure that the ivy did not encroach on the rose's territory and vice versa. It was difficult enough to keep 'New Dawn' manageable on its allotted wall.

The ivy also spread along the north side, a direction I approved of heartily. With judicious snips I kept it off a window, and tried to stop it from climbing over the rooftop parapet. The irksome task of controlling its vertical growth was best accomplished if I walked up to the roof and cut it back from there with my pruners. Onward and upward—generally upward—is the nature of most vines, a genetic imperative that must be kept in check on a terrace that has defined limits.

A few specific remarks about ivy: Boston ivy (*Parthenocissus*) is native to Japan, and grows by affixing sticky pads to a wall; often I use Scotch tape to encourage it to spread laterally until it catches on to the idea. Boston ivy turns red before shedding its three-lobed leaves in autumn. It should not be confused with English ivy (*Hedera helix*), a different genus altogether. English ivy, also from Asia, is an evergreen that is much more tenacious and aggressive, and it can damage old walls by creating fissures with its aerial roots. Boston ivy's sticky pads do not create fissures the way aerial roots do.

Unfortunately, not everybody understands this distinction. One year a contractor, hired to find the origin of a leak in an apartment below me, surveyed my terrace, gave the Boston ivy a dirty look and started ripping it off the wall with a triumphant yelp. I think he expected the wall to crumble. I may have screamed. The downstairs neighbor sued me for causing structural damage to her apartment. I was threatened with eviction by the building's owner, who was also sued by the downstairs neighbor for not acting speedily to fix her leak. I hired a good lawyer who told me to bring on board a smart engineer. The smart engineer got permission to inspect the downstairs apartment. He poked around and took soundings—and determined that a corroded water pipe in the downstairs neighbor's wall was the source of her leak.

My Boston ivy was exonerated. The craziness and ill will I'd gone through is not unusual for gardeners on city terraces, who are always blamed when there is a leak on a lower floor. I'm not saying we are never to blame; I'm just saying we are always the first to be blamed—and not just for a leak in an apartment immediately below us. During this wretched time in the 1980s, the building was "going co-op" in a plan that allowed renters to stay on; I decided to remain a renter. An interim superintendent was appointed to prioritize an inherited pile of work orders. He was swamped. A fourth-floor tenant I was friendly with told me that when she complained that the water in her toilet bowl was backing up, the exasperated fellow told her to wait, the ivy on my terrace might be to blame.

Decades later the vines were destroyed when their wood boxes had to be carted away for an excellent building-wide upgrade by a new management company. The pitted and cracked concrete surfaces on all of our terraces and patios were dug up, retarred, and replaced by textured pavers. I loved the textured pavers; I still do, but I didn't love the harsh look of my redbrick walls denuded of ivy, so I bought a handsome stone tub at a garden center and started over with new Boston ivy. It has not achieved the majestic breadth of the original planting, and never will; the old ivy was rooted in two deep boxes, not in one tub. Since ivy's favorite habit is to climb upward, I still walk up to the roof, now a landscaped roof garden, to trim back its vertical growth with my pruners.

HONEYSUCKLE IS NOSTALGIA

Who wouldn't want a climbing honeysuckle that cascades over a porch? Achieving that effect in a low polyurethane trough on a city terrace isn't easy, but it can be managed, at least for a few years.

One of the charms of honeysuckle, besides fragrance, is nostalgia. Honeysuckle is mentioned in Shakespeare; honeysuckle bowers are a beloved presence in British cottage gardens and on suburban American porches. Honeysuckle is also a great favorite with children. During my childhood in Brooklyn, pale yellow-and-white honeysuckle covered a chain-link fence along the railroad cut on my dead-end street. The fence kept us from tumbling onto the tracks when a freight train chugged by; the honeysuckle was planted for beautification. Flinging our bodies against the barrier, we'd count the coal cars and wave at the caboose. We always got a wave back. When the tumult was over, we'd pull off some honeysuckle flowers to sip the droplets of nectar. Grownups never engaged in this fun activity; they didn't bounce into piles of autumn leaves either.

Today I know that the sweet-smelling vine of my childhood was Hall's honeysuckle, a rampant, invasive grower introduced here from Japan in the nineteenth century. Hall's honeysuckle has been called an ecological disaster; several states have banned it as a noxious weed.

Honeysuckle reentered my life in a roundabout way while I was tending three yew bushes in redwood boxes on the north side of my terrace. Privacy was the point. Windows often face other windows in big cities, and apartments with terraces often face other apartments with terraces. The yews, a male and two fruiting females, effectively screened my dining room window from the window of the terrace apartment across the way. Fresh light-green needles on the yews were a delight in spring; red berries on the females nourished the birds of autumn. When snow fell on the boughs, or when icicles formed, I had a magical winter wonderland. During the summer, I found the somber dark green hedge oppressive.

A solution presented itself when I read the British gardener and author Christopher Lloyd, who advised that a flowering vine could be coaxed to scramble through a hedge. I crammed the roots of an American honeysuckle, *Lonicera flava*, a well-mannered, yellow spring-bloomer, into one of the yew boxes. The vine threaded and twined, and finding no further upward support, formed a canopy over the yews.

My bower effect required a lot of pruning to keep the yews from extending their reach toward my window, and to keep the scrambling honeysuckle from denuding the yews' lower branches. Even when the honeysuckle was in bloom, I felt hemmed in by the somber yews. Yews go back thousands of years in history. Yews serve as hedges and topiary in formal gardens, as gnarled sentries of illegible tombstones in country churchyards. Anticancer properties have been found in some species. By occupying such a vast amount of space on the terrace's north side, the yews completely blocked my neighbor's view into my apartment, and my view into my neighbor's apartment, but they blocked my view of the sky as well.

I don't remember the year this incident happened, but I recall it clearly: on a warm summer morning I walked out on the terrace with my cup of coffee and got an icky surprise. A loaded condom had made a soft landing into one of the yews during the night. I'd long been resigned to picking up cigarette butts flicked off the roof deck, and I've had the sad task, four times, of removing the stiff bodies, so light, of young birds

'Major Wheeler'

that misjudged their flight patterns and smashed into my living room picture window, but extricating a full condom from the branches of a yew was a singular experience, to put it mildly. With humor that I could not muster, a commiserating neighbor advised, "Think of the positive side! Whoever they were, they were using protection."

At some point after the incident of the condom in the nighttime, my wood boxes of yew and honeysuckle were broken up and carted away so the north parapet could undergo new bricking and pointing. I can't say I was crushed by the loss, which opened hidden vistas of the sky, the river, and the meatpacking district. Less advantageously, the loss reopened the direct views into my neighbor's apartment and mine.

The current neighbor, new to the building, thought I had violated her Magna Carta of rights.

"Don't you always keep yews on your side?" she inquired.

"Not any longer," I answered firmly.

After our freighted but civil exchange, the neighbor across the way tried a variety of screens on her side, most recently a trio of young birch clumps that make me yearn for the birches I used to tend.

On my side, I put in a stand-alone trough of honeysuckle, the bright-red tubular *Lonicera sempervirens* 'Major Wheeler', a noninvasive tireless bloomer with inner touches of yellow that was discovered about thirty years ago on the coast of North Carolina by Patricia Wheeler, a wild flower enthusiast. She named it for her husband, the former president of a North Carolina gardening foundation. I've been working with 'Major Wheeler' for a few years. From my prior dealings with the honeysuckles 'Serotina' and 'Goldflame' at inadequate stations elsewhere on the terrace, I understand that I've given the 'Major' an assignment that severely cramps its natural growing habits.

If 'Major Wheeler' had its druthers, it would grow six feet high and wide. Trained by my green plastic ties, the vine has weaved through and twined up the parapet's wrought-iron railing, flowering nicely, but it has exceeded three feet of vertical growth and is flailing around for additional upward support I can't provide. In its exuberance, the 'Major' marches west on the railing toward the afternoon sun, inching toward the sacred corner that houses my treasured hydrangea 'Nikko Blue'. I stop this incursion in its tracks with my Felco pruner. I'd like the 'Major' to march east, toward a structural wall and my recessed tool shed, but that maneuver goes against its phototropic instincts and requires an enormous number of plastic ties.

Another problem is that the stems of the honeysuckle are bound to thicken over time into unsightly bare wood. This is what happens to honeysuckles. A thick-stemmed honeysuckle may not be a problem if the vine is planted in a yard and you're up on your porch delighting in its flowers and fragrance, but my highrise terrace has only one level. So far 'Major Wheeler' has been easy to trim, but I may have to cut the whole vine back, drastically, in a few years. By "drastically" I mean down to its woody base, a procedure that honeysuckle authorities say will encourage new flowering stems. If I decide against extreme pruning—in essence that means starting over—I'll dig the plant out of its trough and bring in a young 'Major Wheeler'. An ongoing replacement strategy might be the best way to keep this honeysuckle on my porch.

HELPING A CLEMATIS

Have I ever given clematis a decent break? Clematis—pronounced "CLEM-atis"—is a beloved vine for temperate climates that comes in different shapes, sizes, habits, colors, and shades, and with different pruning regulations. The plural of "clematis" is also "clematis." As with many of the plants I grow, I saw my first clematis in a glossy print catalog and was instantly smitten. Wayside Gardens, my bible in my novice years, featured a glorious photo of 'General Sikorski', a large-flowered, purple clematis with yellowish anthers. So I purchased one plant and dug a ridiculously small hole for it in a corner of the wood box on the south side of the terrace that was home to my new peach tree. I understood that most vines grow upward but hoped that with plastic ties along the wrought-iron railing the 'General' would adjust to lateral expansion.

And adjust it did. I gave the 'General' some powdered limestone because I read that clematis prefer alkaline soil. I covered its little corner with bark chips because several authorities insisted that sun-loving clematis need a bark-chip mulch to provide a cool root run. I cut the vine back after its first flowering in the spring, the protocol for clematis in Pruning Group Two, to which the 'General' belonged. I saluted whenever one of its splendid flowers unfurled. Ever the researcher, I bought several books on clematis cultivation, and learned that clematis does not require alkaline soil or a mulch of bark chips, which actually depletes the soil's nitrogen, but it does benefit from deep watering every day to keep its roots cool. When the peach tree died and its wood box was trashed, that was the end of 'General Sikorski'.

'Warsaw Nike' on its trellis

For many seasons, on the north side of the terrace, I tended 'Sweet Autumn' clematis, a splendid grower with small, fragrant, and profuse starry white flowers. Native to Asia, it's often described here as invasive, even thuggish—hey, that's a good recommendation to me. Nervy in those days, I got the 'Sweet Autumn' clematis to climb a sturdy latticed wood frame that was technically outside my terrace's perimeter. Perhaps "technically" needs some elaboration. In those days, this apartment building had a public viewing area that separated my terrace from the terrace of my neighbor across the way, but the viewing area was closed off and fitted with an alarm after some agile thieves learned of its existence.

Anyway, when the north side was gutted to accommodate new pavers, or for the pointing and rebricking—I forget which and do not want to dwell again on disasters—the 'Sweet Autumn' clematis came to its end, though the latticed wood frame is still in place. I wonder if anyone would object if I started another 'Sweet Autumn' clematis on that out-of-bounds wood frame? I don't wish to find out.

To be bereft of clematis gnawed at my gardening soul. Recently, it dawned on me that a pot for a clematis could be jammed on the southeastern end of the terrace where a new stockade fence, attached to a railing, separates my space from an absentee neighbor's. I figured that a modest-sized trellis for the clematis could be drilled into the wall between the fence and my living room window. Some experts say a clematis should not be grown on a wall trellis because the heat from the wall will rob the vine of moisture. I maintain that a wall trellis is the only way to grow a clematis on my windy terrace. Lowe's, the chain store for do-it-yourselfers, delivered a lightweight PVC vinyl trellis six feet tall and twenty-eight inches wide that required only minor assembly. I appreciated its neutral mocha color—I wanted my clematis to be the star, not its supporting frame.

Next on the agenda, obviously, was which clematis to buy. Naturally I thought of 'General Sikorski'. In bits and pieces online I learned about Brother Stefan Franczak, a Polish monk who started tending a Jesuit monastery garden in Warsaw during the 1950s, where he created numerous clematis hybrids, including one he named 'Jadwiga Teresa' for a woman helper. To the monk's fury, 'Jadwiga Teresa' was renamed 'General Sikorski' without his permission when a British distributor released it in the West. Perhaps the new moniker was a ploy for name recognition; the real Sikorski, a Polish patriot, died in a plane crash during World War II. Both names are used interchangeably to identify this clematis today. Bedridden in his final years, Brother Stefan died in 2009. By then the monastery had turned his testing fields into a manicured park.

British hybridizers have dominated the clematis business since the middle of the nineteenth century; the Jackman family of Surrey is particularly well known, but I'd developed an interest in the Polish monk's creations. After much hemming and hawing, I chose his 'Warsaw Nike'—five-inch dark, velvety, reddish-violet flowers with perky golden anthers—that Brother Stefan named for the city's tragic, failed uprising against its Nazi occupiers in 1944. 'Warsaw Nike' is supposedly shorter than 'Jadwiga/Sikorski' and is reputed to do well in a pot.

Most clematis varieties are not natural-born climbers. That is the truth. They do not have sticky pads like Boston ivy and are not vigorous twiners like morning glories. A clematis will attempt to wrap its tendrils around *something*, but that something cannot be wide or thick. Clematis tendrils will wrap around each other with alacrity, strangling their own buds, unless the vine is given a support system—in large gardens that support is usually a nearby shrub. Since my 'Warsaw Nike' has to make do with a PVC trellis with thin, flat slats, it needs lots of plastic ties and vigilant human training. I am doing this faithfully, and so far so good. During its second year it made great strides in climbing the mocha trellis and its dazzling red-violet flowers, blooming in clusters, were indeed five inches in size.

ALAS, THE ROAMING CAT

A British garden writer named Beverley Nichols lovingly described the charming antics of his cats in his backyard. Bully for him and his charming cats. The antics of Christopher, the cat who ruled my terrace for fourteen years, were not charming. He was a terror.

I am a dog person. Tilly, my Arkansas coonhound and boon companion, did not consider the terrace a place of interest unless we were having a cookout; in those years cookouts were still permitted on rooftops and balconies. The morning after we'd feasted on steaks, franks, or burgers she'd circle the charcoal grill and wag her tail to pantomime "Any more meat?" Dogs are truly great pantomime artists among their many lovable qualities.

I was devastated when Tilly died. In my vulnerable state, a friend who was a savior of cats saw an opening. She'd found a kitten on Christmas Eve and asked me to come over, just for a look, because she already had six cats and she'd had to shut this one in the bathroom for his safety. On a trial basis—I was firm about that—I stupidly took home the adorable black kitty that snuggled under my jacket the moment he saw me. I named him Christopher Robin for the Christmas gift from Robin the cat savior, and of course for *Winnie the Pooh*. Within two weeks I knew I had taken in trouble.

Christopher was a wildling not cut out to be a house cat. I didn't understand this at first because I knew little about cats. The first time I opened the terrace door he twitched his nose and pricked up his ears. The second time he made a mad dash for the outside, but I was faster. We played the cat-and-door game often enough for me to see that I had a threefold problem: (1) Christopher was focused like a laser beam on the terrace door. (2) Cats are known to have fallen off a terrace in pursuit of a bird. (3) Cats that have been given home, even on a trial basis, cannot be returned to a cat savior.

I consulted with various cat people about my dilemma. Almost unanimously, they urged me to bring in a second cat so Christopher could have a diversion, an idea that made me shudder. With the exception of one person, everyone agreed that Christopher should not be allowed onto the terrace. A neighbor, a refugee Hungarian fashion designer, gave me her Old World perspective: "Your relationship with your cat cannot be defined by a terrace door," she said in her paprika accent. "He must live his life and you must live yours. If he falls off the terrace, the fall was his fate, his destiny."

I let the cat out. For a while he amused himself by catching butterflies and leaping at bees. Blue jays taunted him from the birches. Once he brought a mourning dove into the house that I managed to free. All too quickly he discovered that four more terraces a cat needed to explore were connected to ours by a series of hedges, fences, and railings that could be surmounted. He added those terraces to his territory. His favorite trick was to balance on the wrought-iron railing of the terrace across the way, within my sight but totally beyond my reach. If he slipped it would be a twenty-floor drop. When he'd notice me watching in fright, he'd perform a circus tightrope maneuver, lifting his paws in a gut-wrenching turn. I could not bear to look. He was enjoying himself, the feral bastard.

And so we began an era, lasting more than a decade, when Chrissie would roam the adjoining terraces, leaping over fences, scooting around hedges, and scratching on the neighbors' windows and screen doors. The cat and I had an understanding: I'd leave a window open during the day so he could always come in, but nights were off-limits. Sometimes he returned from his territorial rounds in such an agitated state that I knew he'd had a scary adventure we both wished he could relate. Dan, my cat-friendly neighbor, would cheerfully ring my doorbell and hand-deliver him (once with a red bow) when Chrissie had driven him crazy by scratching and meowing all morning.

Two neighbors on this floor who did not find cats charming were infuriated by Chrissie's antics and by my disregard for their concerns by letting him roam. They were within their rights, of course. On some floors in this building, cats are not permitted to roam in the hallways, and tenants with cats may not leave their apartment doors ajar because of complaints from neighbors with cat allergies. Collective living is difficult, a continuing effort to refine the rules and keep the peace. Once Chrissie brought me uprooted tulips that were not grown on this terrace. Once he showed Dan a disemboweled mouse fetus. Once he dived through an open window and pooped on a neighbor's bed.

One day he did not come back. Fearing the worst, I searched the perimeter of the building at street level. No cat. No mangled body of a cat. It started to rain. It rained for three days. I grieved for the cat's wretched death. I thought I heard a plaintive meow. "Of course you thought you heard a meow," consoling friends soothed. On the evening the rains ceased, a neighbor on a lower floor opened his terrace door and saw a furry black shape and a pair of glowing eyes in a planter. "A monster's out there," he said to his partner. His partner took a closer look and said, "I'm calling Susan." I came to retrieve Christopher. Gently I picked him up and cradled him in my arms. He stared up at our terrace three floors above, the height he had fallen from but had no way to scale. "Whew, what took you so long?" his expression read.

The vet fitted Christopher with a plaster cast for his broken forelimb. When the cast came off, the cat was gimpy. I decided there would be no more access to the terrace—well, okay, there would be supervised visits with a snug halter around his middle and me holding the leash. Christopher let me know that he'd rather stay inside than suffer such humiliation. So I let him go out the door without the halter but with me hovering beside him. I watched him come to terms with his infirmity and limitations. His high-leaping days were over. For the rest of his natural life he stayed in close range and made do with swatting bees and lunging at my legs. I have the scars to prove it.

THE MOCKINGBIRD ON THE ROOFTOP

The spring of the terrible rains brought an aggressive mockingbird into my life. He was young, wild, and crazy, and he made some bad choices.

Mockingbirds are easy to identify. They are dark grey, about ten inches in length, with a lighter underside and jaunty tail feathers. In flight their large black wings reveal white patches. The birds make some distinctive calls, typically a raspy *chack-chack* and a softer, plaintive *hew-hew*. Ornithologists say that the mockingbird is named for its ability to mimic hundreds of birdsongs. My mockingbird's repertoire was limited to *chack* and *hew* with an emotional pitch that went from cocky to desperate.

Spring is mating season for the territorial mockers, whose flying range is one to three acres. Normally, the male bird constructs a cup-shaped nest of leaves, grass, and artificial fibers—whatever is handy—three to ten feet above the ground in a small tree or a shrub. Then he vocalizes—*chack-chack*—to attract a female to his abode. Nest-making in a protected location, and advertising it, so to speak, is a competitive enterprise for a single male, since mockingbirds are monogamous once they pair up and breed. Pair bonds may last for several seasons.

After a successful courtship, the actual mating takes a few seconds. The male jumps the female on the ground and gets under her tail feathers in an act that is called a cloacal kiss. Rudimentary development of the embryo in the female—tiny concentric layers of yolk, albumen, and shell membrane—is complete in a day or so, and then she must lay. If you think about it, as I have, you will seize on the obvious fact that a pregnant bird could not stay aloft if she's carrying a heavy load. After fertilization, she has precious little time to pad her chosen mate's nest before she lays "three to five tiny pale blue or green eggs blotched with russet or cinnamon," according to those who've seen them, that will mature and hatch in twelve days. The female incubates her egg clutch, and both mockingbird partners handle the feeding chores for the hatchlings. Insects are a favored food. Ten days on, the hatchlings have grown enough feathers to be called fledglings and are ready to practice flying, though the chicks still require protective vegetation while they flap and stumble in their efforts to get airborne.

My mockingbird made his nest inside a metal standpipe on the co-op's landscaped roof deck for sunning and socializing that is directly above my terrace. In his bird brain, my garden was part of his territory "on the ground." A normal mockingbird should have intuited that the roof deck of a Manhattan apartment house was a poor choice for a nest. To his credit, the hapless bird did get some aerial look-sees. One day I walked up to the roof and watched in awe as two, sometimes three, mockingbirds made wide circles in the sky in the competitive stage of mating, but my bird never clinched the deal. Of that I am certain.

Our nasty interactions began one morning when I stepped onto my terrace and the resident mocker swooped down from the roof and flicked me on the shoulder with his wing. I tried to interpret the flick as a friendly nudge, a sort of "I like you, let's play" gesture. When the flicking happened again and again, when he began to *chack*, spread his wings and dive-bomb close to my head every time he saw me—nearly every time I stepped onto the terrace—I realized that he wasn't playing. He wanted to drive me away. "You stop that," I'd scream, stamping my foot, which accomplished nothing. His lightning strikes always ended with a quick retreat to the roof, where he'd perch on the parapet ledge biding his time for another assault. In fairness to the bird, he never used his beak or went for my eyes, but I began to flinch whenever I opened the terrace door.

I flew to the Internet, where I learned it is not unusual for a mockingbird to harass a human it believes is a danger to its nest. I read the story of a postal worker in Tulsa who was attacked daily by a mockingbird on her delivery route. I downloaded a University of Florida study on the uncanny ability of mockingbirds to remember and harass specific humans while others, deemed less threatening, were given a free pass. I discovered that mockingbirds have many detractors and many supporters. Atticus Finch in Harper Lee's *To Kill a Mockingbird* was a very articulate supporter. All the information I gleaned was helpful, especially when I learned that my misery would end at the conclusion of the mating season. In a mockingbird's best scenario, the breeding cycle is completed in slightly less than one month. In an adverse scenario when there is no mating, a loser mockingbird flies off in defeat.

Early one morning I stepped onto the terrace and realized it was the second morning in a row without a mockingbird assault. Emboldened, I walked up the flight of stairs to the roof deck to search for the nest.

Melisandra, an artist who lived in the building, was sitting in a deck chair, looking grim. She spent hours on the roof, day and night, to smoke and converse with her private demons. "Did you tell anyone about the nest?" she asked.

"Me? No. I came up to look for it. Wow, Melisandra, that mockingbird must have given you a really hard time."

"I'd just move to another chair."

"Melisandra, can you show me where the nest is?"

She sighed, and walked me to an open standpipe decorated by tin latticework and partially covered in vines. The nest was inside the standpipe. I felt it gingerly with my fingers. I couldn't feel any signs of occupancy whatsoever.

"It's a very clever nest," she said wistfully. "The fledglings flew away while I was gone for two days."

"There were no fledglings on this roof deck," I snapped, more harshly than I intended. "And the nest was not clever. The landscaper who covered the pipe with latticework and a vine was clever, but he couldn't have predicted what happened."

I was sorry to puncture Melisandra's illusions, but that fool of a mockingbird was an idiot. No sensible female would have laid her eggs in that spot.

FALL IS FOR RECKONING

The days are getting shorter, there's a nip in the air, and the plants on my terrace are reacting to the seasonal change. Bright red leaves flutter off the Boston ivy; the honeysuckle is dropping mottled foliage that last week, I swear, was vivid green. At twenty floors above the street, my garden responds to the advent of autumn two weeks before the neighborhood gardens in real ground. Up here the wind has already chased fallen leaves into piles behind the big corner tubs and under my wood table and chairs. I will sweep the debris into large plastic bags that I'll shove down the compactor chute in the hallway. And I'll repeat this chore again and again as autumn proceeds to close things down.

A chore that I won't do is mulching. Does that sound like unmitigated laziness? I'll say it again: I will not mulch my plants in an effort to protect them from a cold winter, erratic freeze/thaws, and fierce winds that might heave a plant's crown above the soil line. Early in my gardening career—I mean my consuming hobby—I noticed that winter mulches do not stay in place on a windy terrace. Wood chips and pine needles, the usual suggestions, blow away. If nature provides a snow cover this winter, I will be grateful, but snow is the only help my plants are going to get. Sink or swim is my motto.

Not everything is moving toward closure, not yet. Freed from their summer doldrums, the roses put on a fall show. 'Nathalie Nypels', the Dutch wonder, has sent up a perky display. A strong new cane of the Canadian 'William Baffin' emerged from the soil a couple of months ago to climb its wall with vigor. By tying in the cane every twelve inches I've trained it to slant horizontally so lateral flowering branches will form next spring. The fall flower show on the other roses has been less spectacular this year, but the bushes have orange hips, round or oblong (depending on the rose) for autumn color.

Damn it, I thought I'd swept up all the shards of green glass from the Heineken bottle! This is horrible! A week ago somebody on the roof deck dropped the empty bottle between the lavender and a hydrangea during the night. The next morning I saw the large fragments and the tiny pieces. I have no idea who dropped the bottle, a tenant in this building or a guest, but I'd like to grind that person's face into the shattered specks I'm still picking out from between the pavers. This bottle did not drop accidentally. It was an act of class warfare by someone probably very drunk, and obviously very hostile.

I understand where the rage comes from. It's the rage of the less privileged against the privileged. The co-op board has rules defining how residents and their guests should comport themselves on a communal landscaped roof garden with a 360-degree view. A big NO sign on the roof's door reads "No smoking, no dogs, no grilling, no glasses, no bottles, please use paper cups and deposit them in the trash bins, roof closes at 10 P.M., respect your neighbors," etc. These rules are usually honored in the breach.

All the benches and chairs for sunning during the day and socializing at night are in a recessed area above my terrace. If you're reading fast, I'll repeat that: All the rooftop's benches and chairs are above my terrace. If folks wish to look down from the parapet, they must climb into a planter or push through a hedge. A surprising number of people do this. If they resent rules and regulations, or are blotto, or both, and they see a garden without a bunch of restrictions, it is a target for flicking a cigarette butt, plopping a soda cup, and on one memorable occasion, lobbing a full condom to see where it lands.

When I started my horticultural adventure I naively believed that people on the rooftop would appreciate a peek at a secret garden. Secret gardens were devised by rich landowners in the Middle Ages to keep out poachers, and by monks wanting a retreat for undisturbed contemplation within the grounds of a monastery. Hidden enclosures, or "rooms," became an artful feature of the elegant estate garden, and eventually terraces on highrises became an integral part of the big city's landscape. Frances Hodgson Burnett's rhapsodic 1911 children's novel *The Secret Garden,* still in print, is all about the thrill and romance of discovery.

Today people bristle, quite rightly, at the unfair privileges of others. So do I; I am not in the one percent of the population that controls the world, and my terrace should not be a symbol of the haves versus the have-nots. I've been living in the same place and gardening happily for thirty-five years because of the city's laws on rent stabilization. I pay less than market value, though my rent goes up every two years while my income goes down, as it usually does for older people. One day the landlord lobby will end rent stabilization, so I worry a lot about the future. Where would I go if I have to leave? I should not be a target for a cowardly bottle dropper in the dead of night who does not understand real class warfare in privileged Manhattan where it's nearly impossible to get a decent apartment unless you are rich or have rich parents.

Here's a backstory I invented for my bottle dropper: Rich parents finance a small "unit" ("unit" is realtor speak) in the building for their spoiled kid who was living at home after leaving college. The kid discovers that scrounging for a job in this economy is a bummer—but thinks a brazen act that dumps misfortune on somebody else is cool and funny. End of story. It's not about me at all.

My quirky orange gazanias, so slow to open in the morning, are still blazing. Gazania must be treated as an annual in this climate, so it will stay in its station until it expires from the cold. Speaking of orange, the annual marigolds are not ready to quit either.

In the department of purple, a welcome color in any season, the annual salvia and the perennial campanula are slowing down, and so is the buddleia. The buddleia's trusses are half the length of its summer trusses, yet sufficient to still attract a hungry bee. The clematis vine is sporting five new velvety flowers, hallelujah. I wasn't sure it would take to the slatted wall trellis I bought for it two years ago.

The dwarf geraniums seem unaware that a frost might overtake them. Four little 'Telstars' from Mrs. Lorraine Smith in Maine have formed one mass of cardinal-red blooms in their pot beneath the buddleia's purple trusses. A pot of salmon minis, my thirty-year friends, is now beyond reach of the setting sun. Soon I must dig out all the geraniums, untangle and trim their roots, and pot up individual plants in fresh soil for their winter sojourn on a sunny shelf below my bedroom window. That shelf will be crowded—it already holds tiny geranium cuttings that I rooted and potted during the summer— so I'll need to employ the window ledge in my living room for the geraniums as well.

Yellow: my sort-of field of golden coreopsis performed valiantly this year. I'm thrilled that the bees that harass the flowers are near the end of their annual invasion. 'Little Lemon', the dwarf goldenrod, has managed a few final lemony tufts.

In the culinary department, the chives, parsley, and basil are still going strong. The chives are perennials and will return in the spring. Parsley is a biennial, which means it will return with a flourish next spring and then die and be replaced. Basil is an annual, period. When a serious frost comes, its end will be swift. For now I feel a responsibility to keep drenching its pot with gallons of water, but I doubt that I'll make any more pasta a pesto this year; there's a limit to how often my poker and mah-jongg groups wish to consume my homegrown specialty. Basil, begone already!

The daylilies are long gone; they finished blooming at the end of July, though the clumps still need watering, and vigilant watching to remove errant seedlings that sneak into their pots. The honeysuckle 'Major Wheeler' that blessed me all summer with red trumpets is ready to retire; I must say the 'Major' did so well this year that I needed to halt its march into the territory of 'Nikko Blue' the hydrangea. The two pots of mexicali penstemons, one purple and one cerise, are still producing flowers if I snip off the depleted stems. A penstemon seedling rooted between two pavers near its mother-plant, the one with the cerise bells; its slender leaves were unmistakable. I pulled the seedling, plunked it into a three-inch pot of fresh soil, and brought it indoors. If the volunteer survives (iffy, iffy), I'll happily plant it outdoors next spring and see what happens. No need to give any thought to the portulaca volunteers that are still popping up hither and yon; they will appear again in various places next summer, and I'll let the prettiest ones stake their claims.

In previous years I've done some serious fall planting (peony, iris) when it was called for. This autumn I'm restricting myself to one pot of six narcissus bulbs. It's been a long time since I bothered with bulbs. Will they come up in the spring? Guess I'll find out.

Autumn is a time of reckoning, a sizing up of what met my expectations and what didn't and probably never will. (I doubt the edelweiss will be a keeper.) Autumn is heralded in late September in the northern hemisphere by the harvest moon, a big pumpkin in the sky that rises before sunset, an astronomical effect of the autumn equinox caused by the Earth's rotation around the sun on a tilted axis. The harvest moon keeps the sky bright when it should be dark, unless the sky is overcast. By legend, farmers celebrated the harvest moon for allowing them extra hours of light in the field to bring in their crops.

It's the most famous moon in the calendar; I try never to miss it from my privileged view.

Autumn proceeds in starts and stops, subject to the phenomenon we call Indian summer, but it is generally in full sway by mid-October or November. Spring's arrival is equally fitful, with a huge difference.

Spring is a time of renewal, universally anticipated and joyously greeted in temperate climates, while autumn's approach signals an end. I can't put a better face on autumn from my perspective. There is much ado in the countryside about the glorious turning of the leaves, but the chief manifestations of autumn in a big city are the sanitation trucks and their crews that collect the fallen leaves from the street trees to prevent them from clogging the municipal sewers. And of course one sees the appearance of jackets and sweaters on the city's population as it hurries about its business.

Oh! Here's a sound I haven't heard in ages: the nightly chirping of crickets. It begins approximately at 9 o'clock and lasts for a few intense hours. Actually the crickets are not chirping—the males are rubbing their wings together and the clatter is their mating call; the silent females apparently know which sounds they prefer.

Crickets also herald the coming of autumn, even in a big city, but why have they arrived on my terrace this year after a long hiatus? I have no idea. Maybe they've lost some of their old habitats in the city? With all the new construction going on in this neighborhood, and all around town, habitat loss for crickets is a reasonable assumption. The sound reverberates on the south side of my garden, but I can't tell precisely from where. Are the crickets lurking in the 'Nathalie Nypels' roses? Are they hiding in tiny cracks in the concrete that anchors the wrought-iron railing? I can't find a trace of the little critters during the day, but it's a treat to hear them in the evening.

The truth is, I'm as tired as some of my plants. The truth is, I welcome a relief from dragging my hose hither and yon. I am ready to pack it in.

EPILOGUE

A Woman's Way

One summer day, the editor of a women's magazine visited my garden with her assistant. They were preparing a feature on how the busy new woman allocates her time, or something like that. My golden coreopsis was looking particularly lush; I pointed to the row of troughs with pride.

"And every month the gardener comes in and changes the flowers?" the editor prodded.

"I'm the gardener!"

She was crestfallen. The busy new woman she had in mind would delegate garden work to others. To "people." As the editorial team made a hasty departure, I heard the assistant mutter, "She hasn't changed her look, either."

That was catty.

Here is another story: On a rare trip to a manicurist I apologized for my rough hands, and explained that I had been gardening.

"Rough hands are a small price to pay for a garden," the manicurist sighed. Now, that was a smart woman.

Dirt under the fingernails, rough hands, and scratches on arms and legs are the routine occupational hazards in a gardener's life. I do not wear gloves when I plant roots—I need to untangle and spread their growth in their newly dug holes before I cover them in fresh soil, tamp them down, and give them a bubbling drink of water. After many hurtful engagements with thorns, I wear long gloves and long sleeves when I prune the roses; rubberized gloves are the best. For general work—adding manure or fresh soil, dragging the hose, weeding, pinching, and snipping, I'm usually in clothes that I don't mind getting dirty. A wide-brimmed hat shields my face from the sun, and if the wind sends it flying I put on an old rain hat with drawstrings that tie under my chin. Add my eyeglasses and you get the picture: not glamorous. I should have worn that rain hat on a long-ago spring day when I shook the yews to rid them of winterkill and a shower of dead needles fell into my hair.

Old shoes are so obvious for garden work—why am I bringing up the subject? E. B. White's emotion-laden preface to Katherine White's *Onward and Upward in the Garden* will do the explaining. His meticulously organized wife, the *New Yorker*'s fiction editor who died before her book was published, would forget she was wearing her good Ferragamos when the impulse to get down in the muck of their New England spread overtook her. But of course! When the impulse to garden strikes, you garden!

Barring the occasional hornworm or beetle, I am the least attractive presence in my oasis when I'm working in it. It is the garden's mission to look fantastic, not mine, yet I admit that when I'm suited up for my chores, a vision of my eccentric appearance can creep into my consciousness. This is likely to happen when a neighbor calls down a cheery hello from the rooftop, breaking my solitude to remind me I'm on display here as much as my garden.

Do men worry about looking eccentric when they work in a garden? I doubt the thought ever crosses their minds; they do not suffer any counterpart to the judgmental weight of traditional feminine attire. England's influential early-twentieth-century landscape designer and author, the short, stout, myopic Gertrude Jekyll (1843–1932) of Munstead Wood, Surrey, bowed to feminine convention in one regard only: she did not dare to wear trousers when she laid out her

'Nikko Blue' hydrangea

impressionist "drifts of color." Outfitted in a snug cap, a workman's canvas apron with pockets for tools, and a pair of laced-up, hobnailed army-issue men's boots, she kept her lower limbs encased in a full ankle-length skirt while she dug and moved plants and climbed ladders to survey the grounds. What an impediment to mobility that skirt must have been. How the fear of looking mannish must have haunted her esthetic soul.

On one embarrassing occasion early in their productive friendship, the architect Edwin Lutyens, Jekyll's young friend and collaborator—he did the houses; she did the gardens—was steadying a ladder for Bumps, as he called her, when the wind upended her skirt to reveal her undergarments. Lutyens kept his grip on the rungs and averted his eyes, but he told the story. Miss Jekyll was still climbing ladders in a skirt at the age of eighty. Her assistant gardeners knew when to turn their gaze elsewhere, though some did snigger behind her back. Remarkably, Jekyll's army-issue boots achieved an iconic status in the twenty-first century. An oil painting of the boots, and a pair of the boots themselves show up in museum exhibits and on Pinterest. From a recent biography I learned that Miss Jekyll once hand-embroidered a banner for a woman's suffrage society. Hooray for her!

Vita Sackville-West struggled to understand her transgressive desires, as her son Nigel Nicolson revealed in *Portrait of Marriage*, the 1973 stunner that included her attempt a half-century earlier to write a confession of her "dual nature." Violet Keppel, her friend since childhood, was visiting, and Vita put on an outfit that "the women-on-the-land were wearing." Some background may be needed here: during World War I, Britain called for "Land Women" to replace male agricultural workers who'd been sent to the battlefields; the volunteers were issued a set of practical trousers that upholders of tradition protested were a horrific display of cross-dressing.

Vita confessed in her manuscript, "In the unaccustomed freedom of breeches and gaiters I went into wild spirits; I ran, I shouted, I jumped, I climbed, I vaulted over gates, felt like a schoolboy let out on a holiday; and Violet followed me across fields and woods with a new meekness." Vita's exultation was her epiphany—she would not suppress the domineering lesbian side of her nature any longer. Costumed in full drag, she ran off with Violet to Cornwall, Paris, and London, where they registered at hotels as man and wife. It took three years for Harold Nicolson to put a stop to this scandalous threat to their marriage.

The restoration of Sissinghurst, a sixteenth-century castle and garden that had fallen on hard times, became the bedrock of an open marriage agreed to by Vita and Harold, a mild-manned diplomat in the empire's Foreign Service. They would each pursue their same-sex desires—her "muddles" and his "fun"—but Vita would not make another spectacle of herself that damaged his dignity. Violet was blamed for everything that had happened.

Jack Vass, the head gardener at Sissinghurst, oversaw the construction of the Lime Walk, the Yew Walk, the Moat Walk, the Nuttery, and the formal garden rooms including the white one, while Harold and Vita planned and argued over the grand schemes in letters to each other nearly every day. An early photo shows Vita ill at ease as she digs with a long spade in a skirt and stockings; in later photos she poses grandly in high boots and riding breeches. The times were changing. When Vass retired three years before her death in 1962, Vita broke with convention and hired two women as Sissinghurst's head gardeners; they stayed on when Britain's National Trust, organized as a charitable foundation, made Sissinghurst one of its properties.

Frankly, I've never cared for Vita, her noblesse oblige, her books of leaden poetry that won major prizes in class-obsessed England, her overweening self-absorption. From what I've read of the weekly garden columns she wrote for the *Observer*, I'd say she was clueless about gardeners with tiny yards. Not that it mattered. Her readers adored being chatted up by the chatelaine of a grand estate: she dispensed advice from on high that they couldn't possibly use, reported at length on the habits of wayward shrubs, and pulled off clever one-liners: "The truth is probably that most plants are temperamental, except the weeds, which all appear to be possessed of magnificent constitutions."

What did Virginia Woolf see in Vita Sackville-West besides an imposing presence, uninhibited sexuality, and a lavish lifestyle? Obviously something very important, for after two fumbling attempts at sex, the women segued into a lifelong friendship. Virginia recorded in her diary that motherhood made Vita "a real woman" whereas she was "a failure"; she was "a failure" as well next to her sister Vanessa who bore three children. I believe Virginia knew from the beginning that Vita was great material for a novel, and novels, not motherhood, were what truly mattered to Virginia Woolf. She mined Vita's life for the sex-changing hero/heroine of *Orlando*. Vita was flattered—she recognized, as did Leonard Woolf, that the mentally fragile Virginia was a rare genius.

Virginia and her Leonard, the "penniless Jew" with a hand tremor, had a small, leaky house with an orchard in Sussex, a place to retreat from the social whirl of London and their duties at the Hogarth Press; their Bloomsbury crowd lived nearby. The garden at Monks House became Leonard's passion; Vita teased that one could not make Versailles on three-quarters of an acre.

Virginia wrote in a refurbished tool shed at the garden's far end, and when the money from her books started to pour in, her private writing quarters were moved to a substantial lodge on one of their new terraces. There were times, she said, when she walked through the orchard so immersed in her thoughts that she bumped into a tree. She picked apples, made blackberry jam, played bowls with Leonard and their friends on a patch of lawn, and fretted whenever Leonard bought more land to expand the garden. He put in a beehive; she helped bottle the honey.

The sales of *Orlando* helped pay for a part-time gardener, their indoor plumbing, and a heated greenhouse. *Flush*, her whimsical "biography" of Elizabeth Barrett Browning's cocker spaniel, paid for two fishponds. A photo of one of Vita's spaniels was on the cover. Virginia had given up her Edwardian dresses, but she couldn't see herself in the riding breeches or the Turkish pants that Vita favored. The two friends went on a lark to get their hair shingled, but neither cared to dress like a Jazz Age flapper. To resolve the eternal question of feminine-enough attire, the blazing feminist of *A Room of One's Own* and *Three Guineas* chose a long skirt, a baggy jacket, and flat shoes.

Once E. M. Forster was invited to Monks House for a spring weekend. On Sunday, his hosts read the newspapers and then retired to write, informing him that he was on his own until lunchtime. Forster stewed in the garden. Eventually Leonard popped out to cut the dead wood on a buddleia bush. Then Virginia came out and proposed that they take Forster's photograph. "That's a good idea," Leonard murmured, continuing to saw the buddleia. "I'm always losing him in the garden," Virginia said in mock horror. "He's up a tree or behind a hedge." To Vita she wrote, "If only I could remember the names of the flowers, and what Leonard is proud of this summer, it would be like one of Miss Jekyll's old letters, minus the common sense."

Leonard added a second greenhouse to the property; their part-time gardener was hired fulltime. "We are watering the earth with money," Virginia scratched in her diary. By 1924, the income from her books had outstripped Leonard's earnings from his books and editing jobs, but she understood that if she'd married the formidable Lytton Strachey, or any of her early suitors, she might not have written anything. Life with Leonard had given her "pure happiness."

In 1941, when the Nazi blitz came to Sussex, Virginia suffered another of her bouts with madness. Leonard worked heroically, as usual, to monitor her sleep, coax her to eat, and stay out of her way when she became violent and called him her enemy. One day in March when a servant rang the lunch bell, Leonard in the garden thought Virginia was in the house. She was not in the house. She had written him a letter to say she was hearing voices again and could not fight them any longer, and then she'd slipped out and walked to the river Ouse to drown herself in its currents. Leonard found her walking stick. Her body was found several weeks later.

A year after Virginia's death, Leonard surprised himself by entering into a new encompassing relationship. Trekkie Parsons was a painter, beautiful, vivacious, and married. She would not have sex with him, but she deeply loved him and his garden. Leonard was used to complications. Trekkie became his chief beneficiary and the executor of his will. Britain's National Trust took over the management of Monks House and its garden, and opened it to the public.

Nobody did transgressive better than Colette, the most popular novelist and essayist in France during the first half of the twentieth century. After an odd start as the precocious author, barely out of her teens, of the naughty *Claudine* novels that her first husband published under his name, her gender bending was wilder than Sackville-West's. She was equally narcissistic, just as scandalous, and even more exhibitionistic than Vita as she conducted torrid lesbian affairs, toured in a risqué music hall revue with Missy, her highborn, titled, cross-dressing lover, and seduced the twelve-year-old stepson of her second husband, who said he was grateful. Her third husband, Maurice Goudeket, protected her from intrusive admirers like a sophisticated incarnation of Leonard Woolf (coincidentally both men were Jewish).

During her long career, Colette published more than eighty books; Americans know her best for the *Chéri* series and for *Gigi*, the novella she dashed off in the last year of the German occupation of Paris when she was seventy, and that was adapted for the stage and screen in many versions, including a musical. Colette's signature style in her essays and fiction was the outrageous pronouncement, which she'd imbibed from her combative mother, Sido. Her mother's garden, a marvel in their Burgundy village, gave her a lifelong love of nature and horticulture.

Colette knew her plants and flowers—their country names, their botanical names, and the precise moment in different parts of France of their triumphant season. She praised the anemone that "opens all at once, like a parachute seized by a gust of wind." She excoriated the iris "that passes for blue, thanks to the unanimity of a host of people who know nothing about the color of blue." She railed at a shop selling "roses that travel by air" and "stand erect on the end of a disdainful stem, and smell of peaches, tea, and even of roses."

Late in her life, when she lived above the gardens of the Palais-Royal in Paris, crippled by arthritis, immensely obese, and confined to her bedroom, a publisher made her an offer she could not refuse: he would deliver a bouquet or a potted plant once a week, and she would send him her musings that he'd make into a little volume. Between rhapsodies and digressions she wrote that peonies smelled like dung beetles and the vanilla scent of the heliotrope was nauseating. That's Colette for you—crouching as always for a pounce.

The first author to tackle male chauvinism in horticulture head on was an American. Eleanor Perényi was a biographer and magazine editor in New York who had gardened on her husband's estate in Hungary before World War II (he was a baron), and then moved to Stonington, Connecticut, with her son and her mother, a popular novelist of the day. Her *Green Thoughts: A Writer in the Garden* (1981), researched while feminism was roaring, devoted a fierce chapter to the prohibitions, dissuasions, and patronizing remarks women endured over the centuries for their "little hobby" or their grander desires, while the repetitive task of weeding was always encouraged.

And yet, as Perényi argued, women were the world's first planters and cultivators, and today one can find scholarly research on women as inventors of the hoe, the woven produce basket, and other gardening equipment while the names of a few women who hybridized famous roses and daylilies have slowly come to the surface. Perényi suggested that someone should write a full treatise on women's place in gardening history. It hasn't happened.

So, is there "a woman's way" of gardening, and more to the point, is it something to celebrate? Not to keep you in suspense, my answer is no. Physical strength was never one of my attributes, but then, people who garden for pleasure have always employed others to handle the heavy manual labor. I've never cottoned to the theory that women are particularly attuned to nature because of the internal reproductive rhythms of our bodies, nor do I think that "eco-politics" is a naturally female endeavor, though I understand full well that when men wage war, women and nature rank high among the deliberate damage. Especially now that I'm an old lady, I gladly pay others to do the strenuous labor. I am still agile enough to climb ladders, but I would never climb one in a skirt, nor would anyone expect me to. That, gardening friends, is true historical progress.

ACKNOWLEDGMENTS

Susan Duff of the Bresnick-Weil Literary Agency pushed me to finish this book.

Big thanks to Alison Owings for suggesting Rutgers University Press.

Rob Sterbal, Sharon Frost, and Holly Forsman sent me photos of the early garden from their files. Patty LaDuca took an up-to-date author photo.

I am grateful to Fahad Waris and Guillaume LeBourhis for their tech expertise.

ABOUT THE AUTHOR

SUSAN BROWNMILLER is a feminist, journalist, activist, and best-selling author. Her most acclaimed title is *Against Our Will: Men, Women, and Rape*. Her other books include *Femininity, Waverly Place, Seeing Vietnam*, and *In Our Time: Memoir of a Revolution*.